DISTANT MEMORIES

A Brief Return to Osseo

by

Daniel Severson

This Book Printed March 19, 2023
Midnattsolen Publishing Company, Yukon Oklahoma
All Rights Reserved
ISBN: 9798385636945

No part of this book may be reproduced in any form or by any means, including electronic, mechanical, photographic, digital or individual handwriting. To that end, any further dissemination of this book's text to any third party, via any computerized storage or retrieval system or other means, without permission in writing from the author and publisher is strictly prohibited.

ACKNOWLEDGMENT

Acknowledgment is given to Mark Gunderman for his professional assistance in meticulously proofreading the original manuscript. Words alone cannot express my appreciation for his assistance with enhancing the overall quality of my work.

DEDICATION

This book is dedicated to Osseo's most famous resident: a colorful individual named Tommy "Tom Cat" Olson. Tommy is also known to many by his alter ego, Detective Steve McGarrett, Hawaii Five-O. By any name, alter ego or alias, Tommy "Tom Cat" Olson is one of the nicest people that I have ever known.

TABLE OF CONTENTS

Introduction   Page   vi

The Return to Osseo   Page   8
Innocence Lost   Page   30
Ma's Place   Page   47
The City of Osseo   Page   67
Downtown   Page   89
Teenage Wildlife   Page   105
Orange And Black Forever   Page   129

Conclusion   Page   *cxliii*

INTRODUCTION

Distant Memories, A Brief Return to Osseo, is presented to the reader as a series of subjective recollections of various events I experienced while growing up in west central Wisconsin, from my birth in 1959 through graduation from high school in 1977. The reader should not think of *Distant Memories, A Brief Return to Osseo*, as a history book. Readers who are interested in objectively reading about the history of Osseo are encouraged to read *Better Openings, A History of Osseo*, by Don Gilbertson.

The mostly stream of consciousness but sometimes linear format that I followed throughout the book allowed me to first identify a number of locations, events and or situations from my youth, and then share a series of personal recollections that are at least tangentially associated with those specific locations, events and or situations. Throughout the writing process I nevertheless attempted to follow a traditional format that introduces the reader to those various locations, situations and or events in chronological order. However, it was not always practical or possible for me to do so.

Distant Memories, A Brief Return to Osseo, introduces the reader to a number of childhood recollections that center around times spent on my father's dairy farm in Jackson County, Wisconsin. The book then continues with several personal recollections involving my youth and adolescence spent living at my mother's house in Osseo, Wisconsin.

Distant Memories, A Brief Return to Osseo, will undoubtedly contain a few historical inaccuracies. Nevertheless, the reader may rest assured that everything I have written down has been presented as truthfully, accurately and candidly as my memory and the extensive research that I have conducted allows. That said, I have intentionally excluded a small number of experiences that might be unnecessarily embarrassing, and or detrimental to the well-being of various friends and family members who are important to me.

Several of the experiences I have shared in *Distant Memories, A Brief Return to Osseo*, are tender recollections of days gone by; pleasant experiences I would not trade for anything. However, there are other disturbing memories as well; unpleasant experiences that I would not wish upon another individual under any circumstances.

> *Life can only be understood backwards;*
> *but it must be lived forwards.*
> *Søren Kierkegaard*

THE RETURN TO OSSEO

Quite unexpectedly, I received a telephone call from my brother Irvin, on July 10, 2022. He had called to inform me that our oldest brother, Larry, passed away earlier that day. My brother Irvin has always been a man of few words, and I've never enjoyed talking on telephones, so after passing on the news about Larry's death, our conversation soon ended. As I hung up the telephone, I began contemplating whether or not to return to Wisconsin to attend the funeral. Initially, I reminded myself that Larry and I had never been that close and decided not to attend. Had the funeral been held within the normal time frame of a few days, I would not have made the trip back to Osseo. However, his daughter scheduled the funeral for July 19, 2022. Having that additional time to reconsider my plans, I ultimately decided to return to Osseo for Larry's funeral.

The drive from my home in Yukon, Oklahoma, to Osseo, Wisconsin, is nearly 900 miles, and under the best of driving conditions takes at least 12 hours to complete. Nevertheless, I decided to drive the entire distance before checking into a hotel. After saying goodbye to my wife, I departed for Wisconsin on July 17, 2022. As the hours began to pass I started reminiscing about growing up in Osseo, Wisconsin. Initially, my thoughts were about my parents. However, my thoughts soon shifted to my eleven siblings.

My father's name was Norman Henry Severson. My sisters always referred to him as Dad, but my brothers affectionately referred to him as, "the old man." However, whenever my mother spoke of him to me, she always referred to my father as Pappy. Accordingly, that is the honorific I have chosen to use when referring to him. Pappy inherited many of the values and customs his ancestors brought with them when they emigrated from Norway to the United States. However, unlike the vast majority of the usually reserved Norwegian immigrants that came to America, Pappy was a man of fiery temper with little or no tolerance for sloth in any form. He attended a small country school for eight years before deciding to work full-time on his father's dairy farm. At the age of 17, Pappy grew restless and went to work raising chickens in a rural area of Illinois known as Ontarioville.

Not finding chicken farming the adventure Pappy thought it would be, he eventually returned to Wisconsin and went to work as a hired hand for some of the more prosperous farmers in the area. Through hard work and thrift, he was eventually able to save enough money to buy his own dairy farm. However, he still supplemented his farm income by taking on a variety of other part-time jobs. For example, Pappy worked on various crews that were assembled to improve the roads and bridges located throughout west central Wisconsin. He also cut and split firewood that he sold to townspeople in the surrounding communities, including what was at that time the Village of Osseo.

My mother's maiden name was Helen Margaret Hanson. My sisters always referred to her as Mom. However, my brothers and I always addressed her as Ma. As with Pappy, Ma also inherited several of the important values and customs that her Norwegian ancestors brought with them when they immigrated to the United States. But unlike Pappy, Ma was a reserved, stoic woman who seldom raised her voice in anger. I remember her as consistently kind and considerate of other people's wants and needs. Being the Norwegian American that she was, Ma seldom openly expressed her feelings of love and affection. However, it was intuitively understood by those nearest to her that they were loved. As a child, Ma attended a country school known as the Holen School, and she was proud of the fact that she never missed a single day of attendance during those eight years.

After completing the eighth grade Ma stayed with her parents until she turned 16 and moved to Edgeley, North Dakota, where she worked as a housekeeper on her Aunt Nettie's farm. Eventually, however, Ma returned to Wisconsin where she found employment as a housekeeper on the farm owned by my great-uncle Hans Severson. It was while working on that farm that Ma and Pappy met and briefly courted. Norman and Helen Severson were married at the parsonage in Osseo, on April 7, 1936. They started their married lives together on an 80-acre farm located on what is now North Prairie Road in the Town of Garfield.

Growing up, it was intuitively understood that Pappy was the leader of our family, and things always had to be done his way. I remember feeling privileged to deliver his lunches to him whenever he worked in the fields. As soon as Pappy observed me arriving with his lunch box, he stopped the tractor that he was operating, usually his Cockshutt Model 50 Deluxe, stepped down from the machine and sat beside one of the tractor's enormous rear tires. As he ate his simple lunches of sandwiches, cookies, fruit and coffee–lots of piping hot coffee–Pappy shared the most interesting stories of this, that and the other. I don't remember a single one of those stories today, but I remember sitting beside him and listening with undivided attention and interest to everything he had to say.

Pappy frequently used the term, "I'll Fix Your Wagon!" when telling his stories. I can't honestly say that I remember his voice any longer. However, I can still see him as plain as day, sitting beside the rear tire of the Mighty Cockshutt while telling a tall tale to me, his powerful arms moving about with his coffee in one hand and his sandwich in the other. It seemed to me that those visits with Pappy were always way too brief–and it still seems that way to me. However, he was of the opinion that there was too much work to do in a day to sit down for any reason. Except, I choose to believe, when sharing a tall tale or two with a small boy beside his tractor.

Pappy's entire purpose in life centered around farming his land and caring for his livestock. During spring, summer and autumn, when there was a seemingly endless amount of work to be done, he literally ran from one place to another between tasks. For example, Pappy ran from the barn to the house after he finished milking his dairy cows. He didn't run to the house from hunger; he did so to consume his breakfast of bacon, eggs and coffee as quickly as possible before heading out to the fields to work. Pappy was of the opinion that there was too much work to be done to walk from one place to another. To this day he stands alone as the hardest-working man that I have ever known.

There is little doubt in my mind that a part of Pappy's work ethic stemmed from the way he was raised by his parents. There is also little doubt in my mind that part of his work ethic stemmed from the hard times he experienced growing up during the Great Depression. Virtually everyone who lived through those difficult circumstances was required to work hard just to survive. However, what I believe above all else is that his approach to work came primarily from a private place found deep within his existence, an exceptional quality that very few humans possess. Pappy worked to live and lived to work and he died doing what he lived for on June 22, 1966. On that darkest of all the days I have lived, Norman Henry Severson was unmercifully crushed to death while baling hay on his dairy farm. He was 51 years old at the time.

I am the youngest of the 12 children born to Norman and Helen Severson. I am 100% American in citizenship and 100% Norwegian in ancestry. That makes me 100% Norwegian American in heritage by my reasoning. I am also the son of two hardworking and highly successful dairy farmers. As with my parents and all of my siblings, I was born in Wisconsin. How Ma cared for the older children I do not know, but by the time I was born in 1959, the excruciating pain and crippling impact of rheumatoid arthritis had made the task of caring for me all but impossible. Fortunately, I had several sisters who were able to step up and help her out with caring for me.

When Ma was 42 and pregnant with me, she experienced the first symptoms of the debilitating autoimmune disease. Very quickly, rheumatoid arthritis spread to her hands, arms, back, neck, feet, legs and hips. Yet, in spite of her unending agony, Ma did everything in her power to make my childhood as enjoyable as possible. To this day I have a seemingly endless supply of beautiful memories of times spent in her company from the time of my early childhood until the day she passed away.

I fondly remember the way she gently put me to sleep at nap time by ticking her fingernails back and forth beside my ear. She also told me any number of bedtime stories she knew by heart. My favorite–which she told me a hundred times if she told me once–was a Norwegian children's story called, *"The Three Billy Goats Gruff."* There were a seemingly endless number of afternoons when I listened to her voice gently telling me fairytales, always accompanied by the soft ticking sound of her fingernails beside my ear. Ma patiently continued doing so for as long as it took until I eventually drifted off into a peaceful sleep. It was only after she was certain that I was sleeping that she returned to the multitude of chores she had to complete.

I also remember there was always–and I do mean always–a variety of delicious cookies, cakes and pies in the house. She routinely baked Norwegian treats such as *Sandbakkels* and *Rosettes* throughout the year. Then there was Ma's homemade bread made from scratch and kneaded by hand. Ma seemed to be kneading bread every day of her life until Rheumatoid arthritis made that task impossible for her to complete. Ma's homemade bread remains the best tasting that I've enjoyed to this very day. From my perspective at least, that subject is not open for debate.

Even as a child I easily observed that Ma and Pappy were about as different as two people could be. On one hand, Pappy was a man of fiery temper with a penchant for hard work and contempt for sloth in all its forms. On the other hand, Ma was a reserved, stoic woman with an amazing ability to multitask while caring for her children. I'm reasonably certain that Pappy's fiery temper is the seminal trait that he passed on to me and that Ma's uncanny ability to organize is the primary quality that she passed down to me. However, I believe with absolute certainty the most important lesson I learned from them collectively is that there is always honor in hard work but only shame in laziness and sloth.

Pappy believed that hard work was the only proper means of making a living, and he never accepted anything of value from another that he had not earned through honest labor. All of his frugality paid off too, particularly as it pertained to providing for his youngest four children. As previously stated, Pappy was tragically killed while baling hay in 1966. Less than a year later, Ma found it necessary to sell the farm and purchase another house in Osseo. She and her children were only able to survive financially because of the equity Pappy built up over the years through his hard work, thrift and economy.

At the time of his death, Pappy owned 527 acres of farmland free and clear. The same was true for his machinery and livestock, etcetera. From that equity, Ma was able to provide for her youngest children until all of us reached adulthood. Ma was eligible for low-income assistance programs such as free school lunches and food stamps. However, she never considered accepting those or any form of public assistance. It wasn't in her character to accept for free that which she was more than capable of obtaining with her own money. With the wisdom of our ancestors guiding her, she understood that welfare and charity were best left for families with children who were "truly in need of assistance," and not for families that happened to meet some arbitrarily assigned eligibility requirements for financial assistance as established by far-away government bureaucrats.

It was around the time that I crossed over the bridge that leads from Winona, Minnesota, into Wisconsin that my reminiscing shifted from my parents to my siblings. As for Norman and Helen's 12 children, I have always thought of us as belonging to three separate groups of four siblings, with each group raised in decidedly different ways. The first group of siblings consists of Margaret Ann, who was born on December 9, 1936; Dorothy Mae, who was born on June 14, 1938;

Larry Gene, who was born on January 12, 1941; and Irvin Wayne, who was born on August 26, 1942.

My childhood recollections of Margaret are very limited. Margaret graduated from high school and enlisted in the United States Army before I was born. Moreover, she was already married and the mother of her first child before I was born. Margaret married a soldier named Paul Keffer on June 26, 1956, and they had four children together. Paul unexpectedly passed away from a heart attack on March 6, 1965. Margaret married a gentleman named Stanley Caucutt on September 4, 1968, and they had two children together. Unfortunately, Stanley passed away from a heart attack on October 10, 2005.

I have no recollection of my sister Dorothy living on the farm. As with Margaret, Dorothy had graduated from high school and moved away before I was born. She was also married and the mother of one child before I was born. Dorothy married a gentleman named Floyd Maug on June 16, 1956. Floyd drove heavy equipment such as dump trucks and graders for Trempealeau County, and Dorothy worked as a nurse's aid. They also owned and operated a small dairy farm with somewhere between 15 and 20 milk cows. Together they had four children. Floyd passed away from a heart attack on December 15, 1972. Dorothy married William Paulson on September 7, 1974. However, they were later divorced. She later married a gentleman named Arnold "Arnie" Hanson on June 20, 1981. He passed away on July 16, 2015.

I also have no clear recollection of my oldest brother Larry living on the farm. He moved away from the farm in 1962, when I was about three years old. His domestic partner was a woman named Kathleen Ann Davidson. Together, they had three children. After my father was killed, Larry and "Kate" took over the operation of Pappy's farm. Kathleen spent the last several years of her life living at the Osseo Area Nursing Home due to complications associated with Multiple Sclerosis. She passed away on February 15, 1999. Larry's domestic partner during the last 41 years of his life was a gentle woman named LuAnne Cantu. Larry passed away on July 10, 2022.

I also have but one memory of my brother Irvin living on the farm. It is undoubtedly a memory from after Pappy was killed but before my family and I moved to Osseo. One fall day I watched as Irvin and our brother Freddie unloaded several loads of firewood. As I recall, Irvin wanted to stack the pieces of firewood into symmetrical rows whereas Freddie wanted to randomly toss the pieces into a pile. With each load of firewood they brought home, the argument continued. When they finally finished their job there were two distinct halves to the same pile of firewood: one half consisting of neatly stacked rows and another half tossed freely into a pile. Could the two Norwegians have resolved their disagreement any other way?

As a young adult, Irvin enlisted in the United States Army and was stationed in West Germany when Pappy was killed. At that time Irvin received orders to return stateside and was subsequently placed in the Army Reserve. To his credit, Irvin consistently and faithfully helped Ma with the operation of the dairy farm until Ma rented the property to her son Larry and we moved to Osseo. Irvin lived with us in Osseo for a time, and worked full-time as a farm implement mechanic. Irvin married a kind and hardworking woman named Nola Jean Rosenthal, on May 24, 1969. Together they have two children.

The second group of siblings consists of Virginia Arlene, who was born on February 28, 1945; Janice Leone, born on September 24, 1946; Frederick John, who was born on June 8, 1948; and Jennifer Ellen; who was born on May 23, 1950. I have only vague memories of my sister Virginia living on Pappy's farm. What I do remember is that she was a remarkably strong person, who worked in the fields right alongside her brothers. She also excelled at baking and cooking. Virginia left home at 16. After living in a variety of places and working at various jobs, Virginia married a gentleman named Wayne Holte, on May 13, 1967. They have three children. Wayne passed away on May 23, 2022. Today, Virginia lives in Osseo.

My equally limited memories of Janice are that of an older sister who helped with both farm chores and housework. As with Virginia, she left home when she was 16. The person that she departed with was a smooth-talking individual named Wallace "Wally" Moyle. Together, they had six children before getting married on May 19, 1973. Sadly, Wally was killed in a snowmobiling accident on January 19, 1975. Some years later, Janice married a man named Michael Cousino. However, they later divorced. She then married a man named Kent Annis, but they also divorced. Janice passed away after a difficult and courageous battle with emphysema on August 30, 2013.

My memories of Freddie are nearly as limited. One beautiful memory I have of him is that once, when I ran out to meet my siblings as they returned home on the school bus, Freddie grabbed me and picked me up in his arms. He then ran home while swinging me about in his arms as though I were an airplane flying in the sky. I also have a fragmented memory of Freddie walking around in the snow on a pair of handcrafted stilts. What makes the memory remain close to me to this very day is that the stilts made it appear as though he was floating above the snow instead of walking through the snow. As with Larry, Irvin, Virginia and Janice, Freddie dropped out of high school. He worked at various jobs until he was old enough to enlist in the United States Marine Corps. Private Severson was stationed in California when Pappy was killed. Freddie received an honorable discharge and returned to Osseo. At some point, he became involved in a romantic relationship with a woman that resulted in the birth of a child. Denise Sue Anderson was born on June 2, 1967. DNA testing completed on May 18, 2012 confirmed that she is Freddie's biological daughter. Fredrick was tragically killed in a one-car accident on August 5, 1967.

The third group of siblings is the family members I vividly recall growing up with–both on Pappy's farm and later at Ma's place in the City of Osseo. Their names are Gloria Diane, born on February 1,

1953; Jeffrey Allen, born on January 23, 1955; Deloris Irene, born on January 20, 1957; and myself. The group of siblings I belong to had a significantly more comfortable home life–in terms of our physical surroundings. However, unlike the first two groups of siblings, we grew up without the benefit of our father interacting with us. We also shared the decidedly unpleasant experience of watching our mother's health deteriorate before our very eyes from the debilitating effects of severe rheumatoid arthritis.

I only have one clear memory of Jennifer living on the farm, and it has always brought a smile to my face. The memory is from an incident when she got bucked off one of the Shetland ponies our Pappy had purchased. Specifically, a mean-spirited firecracker of a pony called Colonel. I was standing on the concrete steps located at the front door to the house when the incident unfolded. Gloria and Jeff were riding their ponies in the front yard and apparently Jennifer decided she wanted to ride her pony as well. At the time she was a little heavy in the bottom. So rather than mount her pony from the side as most people would do, she thought it might be easier for her to get on him from the steps. Specifically, by jumping off the concrete steps onto the pony's back.

Unfortunately for Jennifer, when she jumped on Colonel's back, she startled the pony. In response, Colonel started bucking furiously and caused Jennifer to fall. As Jennifer fell, she landed flat on her butt! I remember laughing so hard that tears formed in my eyes. As with all but one of her older siblings, Jennifer moved away from Pappy's farm while still a teenager. Eventually, she married a person named Leon Darrow on November 14, 1970. They had one daughter. Jennifer and Leon later divorced. Jennifer married a gentleman named Donald Thompson on July 23, 1977. Sadly, Donald passed away from a heart attack on January 20, 2006.

My sister Gloria is six years older than me. When I was a young boy, I thought of her as someone who was superior to me in nearly every way. She certainly knew a lot more about nearly everything than me. Gloria was physically and mentally strong, highly intelligent and a hardworking individual. Unfortunately, she also possessed the same fiery temper as our father. As a result, we seldom got along. Gloria graduated with honors from the Osseo-Fairchild High School in 1971. She later married a gentleman named Jeff Paulson. The couple were married at Ma's place in Osseo on March 22, 1975. For several years they owned and operated a successful agricultural business in Osseo. They do not have any children.

Jeff is the closest of my brothers to me in age. Although he is only four years older than me, he always demonstrated such maturity that I grew up thinking of him as more of an adult than a child. As with our father, Jeff lives to work and works to live. He graduated with honors from the Osseo-Fairchild High School in 1973. Jeff has married and divorced a woman named Gail Linda Smith two times. They first married on August 17, 1974. The marriage ended in divorce. They married a second time on February 15, 1982. However, the second marriage ended in divorce as well. They have three children together.

The desire to farm has always been with Jeff, and he has been a dairy farmer his entire adult life. However, both his life and his livelihood almost ended on August 27, 1994, when an F3 tornado struck the area and completely destroyed his dairy barn. The tornado struck during milking time and killed nearly every animal inside the barn. Only Jeff and his loyal dog Milton survived. Although Milton managed to escape, Jeff was trapped underneath the collapsed barn for several hours before local rescue personnel arrived and extracted him from the building. The tornado was a major setback. However, rather than quit farming, Jeff started rebuilding almost immediately. Over time Jeff was able to reestablish himself as a successful dairy farmer.

Lastly, there is my sister Deloris. As a teenager, Deloris found herself spending most of her free time caring for Ma. She consistently met her responsibilities with a maturity that was well beyond her young age. Deloris learned to speak German in high school and traveled to Germany, Austria and Switzerland with several of her classmates. As part of the European itinerary, she visited several famous locations such as Neuschwanstein. Deloris graduated from high school in 1975. She later married a man named Rodney Johnson at Ma's place, on September 24, 1977. They later divorced. Deloris married Joseph Norris on June 30, 1989. They later divorced. She married James Wirth on October 15, 2019. Deloris does not have any children.

Eventually, I arrived in Osseo for the funeral. Exhausted from the drive, I immediately checked into a hotel room and after unwinding for a few minutes, went to sleep. The following morning, one day before Larry's funeral, I decided to drive out to the cemetery where he would be buried the following day. I parked my car alongside County Road B and walked directly to the gravesites where my sister Janice, my brother Freddie, and my parents were buried. I knew full well that Larry was going to be buried beside them the following day, and that someone would eventually dig the grave where he would be laid to rest. When I arrived I was pleased to find that the ground beside the existing graves had not yet been disturbed. I did not want to pay my respects to them in the presence of an open grave....

After spending a considerable amount of time at the cemetery, slowly walking around its peaceful grounds and stopping at the places where my paternal grandparents, great-grandparents and several other people whom I remembered from my youth were buried, I decided to drive out to the property that was once Pappy's farm, but where Larry had lived since 1967. The farm is accessible by taking one of two gravel roads that extend to the south from County Road B. Today the two roads are called Rindahl Valley Road and South Prairie Road, but I'm not sure they had names when I lived there. After turning to the right, or south onto one of the gravel roads, a visitor will continue driving until reaching Telemarken Road. At that time the driver will again turn to the right, or south, and continue a short distance further down Telemarken Road until reaching the driveway that leads to the farm.

As I drove up to the house where Larry had lived, I wasn't the least bit surprised to find the dirt driveway in the same terrible condition it had always been in. It occurred to me that Larry had rented the farm from Ma since 1967, and purchased the entire property from her as far back as 1977. As I drove down the driveway I thought to myself that Larry hadn't made a single meaningful repair to the uneven driveway in the 55 years that he lived there. After reaching his modest house, I parked my car, stepped out and slowly walked up to the front door of the relatively new building. The original house, the one that I lived in from the time of my birth until 1967 accidently burned to the ground in 1993. Shortly after that happened, Larry hired a gentleman named Marvin Hong to build the current house.

I had only been inside the newer house a couple of times, and from a purely subjective point of view, it never really seemed as though it belonged there as far as I was concerned. Larry had a difficult time adjusting to the new house as well, I suspect. He brought in a small trailer to live in while the new home was being built. However, Larry continued living inside that tiny trailer quite awhile after construction was finished. When I arrived at the front steps, I knocked on the door, fully expecting his domestic partner, LuAnne Cantu, to appear at the door. However, nobody answered. LuAnne was either sleeping or out and about somewhere, seeking comfort with friends or family.

As I turned and walked away, I glanced scornfully at the crumbling outbuildings surrounding me. Although I was gazing out at the same place where I lived the first seven years of my life, from May 1959, until May 1967, the farm didn't look the least bit like the place I remembered. As I looked upon the omnipresence of decay that was once Pappy's handsome farm, I drifted back in time to my childhood. When Pappy owned the place, everything was kept neat, orderly and clean. The buildings were always painted, the fences were taut and everything was in its place. Instead of seeing the outbuildings in ruin, I saw them as they were in 1966, with a common area surrounded by a series of well-maintained outbuildings.

The first building that stood immediately to the right of the driveway was the actual farmhouse. The home that my family and I lived in was a modest but well-maintained wooden structure that was painted white with red trim. Directly behind the farmhouse stood a small orchard with eight or nine healthy fruit-bearing trees. On the left or north side of the farmhouse was a marshy area where domesticated geese and ducks lived. The marsh originated on another of Pappy's four farms called the Call place, and continued in a northwesterly direction until forming Rindahl Creek, which then fed into the South Fork Buffalo River as it meandered along its way until reaching the City of Osseo and beyond.

That marshy area beside our farmhouse provided sanctuary for several wild animals including snapping turtles and muskrats. Whether fact or Severson family legend I cannot say, but the story was repeatedly told when I was a child of an instance where my brother Freddie had an encounter with an angry beaver in that marsh, which resulted in the beaver's untimely death. I do remember Pappy finding it necessary to kill the snapping turtles that found their way into the swamp with the intention of killing his ducks, geese, ducklings and goslings that lived there. I watched once as he speared a large snapping turtle to death with an iron wrecking bar. Curiously, after killing the snapping turtle, Pappy leaned the wrecking bar against a fence with the dead reptile still attached to it. He then left that dead snapping turtle there for several days before someone finally disposed of the rotting carcass.

The farmhouse did not have a basement. Instead, there was only a cellar that was used for storing items. The cellar and foundation were constructed of dark sandstone rocks and mortar. There were several shelves along the walls in the cellar, and that was where Ma stored the canned fruits and vegetables that she and her daughters prepared each year. The cellar was always dark, musty and festooned with a lot of cobwebs. As a small child, I was convinced the place was haunted and remember being frightened to go down there whenever Ma told me to fetch a jar of food for her. I always did exactly as I was told, but I never enjoyed doing so. I remember slowly walking down the creaky wooden steps, grabbing whatever it was that Ma wanted, and then running back up the stairs as fast as my little feet could move!

The farmhouse was a two-story dwelling with two bedrooms upstairs and two more downstairs. The kitchen had wooden cupboards that were painted beige. There was a wood-burning stove in the kitchen that was used for heat in the wintertime, an electric oven for cooking and baking, a refrigerator and a large sink for washing dishes. The kitchen's centerpiece was a rectangular-shaped table with chairs made of solid oak. The table was large enough for everyone in the family to sit down together at mealtime. Even as a young child, I could appreciate the distinctive character of that table. Perhaps it was the table's strength and durability, coupled with its stark simplicity and worn surface that made it so appealing.

To the back of the kitchen was a modest, seldom-used living room with a larger wood-burning furnace used to heat the entire house in wintertime. Directly above the wood-burning furnace was a large, cast iron vent in the ceiling, and through that vent passed all of the warm air that was going to warm the people sleeping upstairs on all of those cold winter nights. Needless to say, heavy, homemade wool quilts were used for additional warmth during the coldest months of the year. The wool quilts were not at all similar to the comforters that are used today. What I remember is that the handmade quilts were heavy, very heavy. Once my brothers and I snuggled in beneath one or more of them for the night, there wasn't much movement until it was time to get out of bed the following morning. Then, once we crawled out of our beds in the morning, we were instantly awakened by the cold, crisp morning air that always jarred away any sleepiness that remained.

My older siblings grew up without television. However, by the time I was born, the family had a small black-and-white RCA television set in the living room. In those days there were two television channels: Channel 13, which was an NBC affiliate from Eau Claire, Wisconsin, and Channel 8, a CBS affiliate from La Crosse. Occasionally, there was a snowy signal received from Channel 7, an ABC affiliate from Wausau, as well. My most vivid memories of time spent in the living room are those rare occasions when the Beatles appeared on *The Ed Sullivan Show*. I'm not really sure why I retain such vivid memories of their appearances after all these years. Perhaps it was their unusual haircuts that makes me remember. Then again, it hopefully has more to do with how talented they were as entertainers.

I also remember watching *Captain Kangaroo* throughout the week on our black-and-white television set. *Captain Kangaroo* was one of the first childhood programs to air on television. Ma was busy doing her various chores around the house every morning, and I spent my time watching *Captain Kangaroo*. As I recall, he told the most interesting stories. He and his friend Mr. Green Jeans conversed about countless subjects that were interesting to me at the time. My favorite part of the show were the appearances by Bunny Rabbit, a hand-held puppet. How Bunny Rabbit managed to get those carrots from the Captain remains a mystery to me to this very day.

"Welcome to the 'Treasure House' boys and girls"
Captain Kangaroo

As previously stated, the dirt driveway leading to Pappy's farm ended with a common area that was surrounded by a series of outbuildings. Among them was a woodshed, granary and toolshed. I loved playing inside the woodshed as well as climbing on top of the woodpile. Jeff was always good to me when we lived on Pappy's farm. However, I can't really say the same about myself. One day, when I was only a five-year-old boy, I shot Jeff in the leg with his own BB gun. As was frequently the case in those days, I spent my time alone at play while Jeff worked with Pappy. On that particular day, I was standing on top of a large pile of wood that was stacked in front of the woodshed and shooting at various things with his BB gun. When lunchtime arrived, Jeff returned from wherever he was working and headed towards the farmhouse. At one point he noticed I was using his BB gun without permission and yelled, "Put that Goddamned BB gun back right away, Danny! I never gave you my permission to us it."

Jeff's yelling not only angered me, it pissed me off! So in response, as Jeff walked passed me towards the front entrance of the farmhouse, I cocked the BB gun and aimed it directly at him. Then, without the slightest hesitation whatsoever, I shot Jeff in the back of his leg, well above the knee. In truth, the target I was aiming for was a bit higher up. I had every intention of shooting Jeff right in the ass! I can still remember how he howled in pain when the BB struck him in the back of his leg. When I heard Jeff howl in pain I prepared for the pounding that I fully expected to follow. However, it never came. Jeff didn't retaliate against me for shooting him in the leg with his own BB gun. Instead, he limped inside the house, had his lunch and then returned to where he had been working. To this day I cannot say why he never exacted some type of revenge on me, but I'm grateful that he did not.

After the woodshed stood the granary. Then there was the toolshed. Although the toolshed was strictly off limits to me, I spent countless hours inside that building digging around in what I thought of as a veritable treasure trove of odds and ends that were interesting to me. The toolshed contained straps of leather, spools of twine, buckets, screws, tools, bolts, nuts, ropes, whatchamacallits, thingamajigs and doohickeys of all sizes and shapes. I loved digging around inside the toolshed, and did so all the time when I was a child–but never with Pappy's permission.

Next in the series of outbuildings was the milk house and after that was the dairy barn. As with nearly all of the outbuildings, Pappy's dairy barn was painted red. A good distance behind the dairy barn were Pappy's pigsties. A pig is truly a filthy animal and their sties are nasty places. It was primarily for that reason that Pappy built them a good distance from the dairy barn and other outbuildings. In spite of their omnipresent stench and filth, I have several fond memories of playing in and around those pigsties. One day a neighbor kid named Mark Leer stopped by for a visit with my brother Jeff. Eventually, the three of us ended up having a BB gun fight in those pigsties. I can only imagine how displeased Ma had to have been when we later attempted to enter the farmhouse covered from head to toe in pig shit.

Directly beside the dairy barn was a small horse barn, and adjacent to that was a tractor shed. My best friend in those days was my sister Dorothy's son, Brian Maug. I always looked forward to those times when Brian visited Pappy's farm. Brian and I played a game inside the tractor shed that we called "Dust Horses." We had hobby horses and rode them around inside the tractor shed. As we rode around on our hobby horses, we kicked up dust and yelled, "Dust Horses!" As simple as the early childhood game sounds, those times spent with my friend Brian Maug are some of my favorite childhood memories of times spent on Pappy's farm. After the tractor shed was the chicken coop and then a garage where Pappy kept his car, a white 1964 model Chevrolet Bel Air with a red top.

In addition to the outbuildings described thus far, there was another building that meant more to me than any of the others. It was quite a bit smaller that the other outbuildings and black in color rather than red. The building sat directly in front of the farmhouse, but outside the fence that surrounded our yard. It was the doghouse where our two dogs lived. I spent a lot of time inside that building with my two best friends, a couple of mongrel dogs named Mike and Sam. Mike was the smaller of the two, with shaggy, reddish-brown colored hair. Sam was the larger of the two, with shorter, light-tan colored hair. He was also a lot younger. I loved both Mike and Sam but was closer to Mike, who was exceptionally friendly and a pleasure to be around.

As previously stated, my oldest sister Margaret's husband passed away in 1965. Margaret and her four young children came to stay with us that summer. As a six-year-old, I had little appreciation for the difficulties my sister was experiencing in her life. What I was aware of was the fact that after the Keffer kids arrived, I had three new friends to play with virtually every day. We did a lot of things together that summer. Things were even better whenever my sister Dorothy stopped by to visit with her two children, Brian and Doug. Whatever kind of play the Keffer kids, Maug boys and I imagined, be in rolling around in the hay barn or running through Pappy's fields of crops, we engaged in it throughout the summer.

Other than that one summer when the Keffer kids lived with us, I spent most of my childhood playing alone. On one such occasion, I wandered away from the farmhouse and got lost. Eventually, Ma noticed I was missing and sent everyone out to the fields to look for me. Fortunately, my brother Larry eventually found me sleeping in a field a short distance away from the farmhouse. Larry then picked me up and returned me to my mother's waiting arms. That wasn't the only time I found myself in a situation where I needed help from an older relative either. When I was young, I enjoyed spending time in the barn while Pappy and my older siblings were busy milking and tending to the cows. While there, I sometimes got into mischief of one form or another.

In the springtime, when Pappy's cows were first let out to pasture, they invariably found themselves grazing on fresh grass for the first time in several months. In response to their new surroundings, the cows tended to gorge themselves on the fresh, tender plants before them, and that in turn led to their experiencing severe diarrhea. On one such spring morning–after Pappy's dairy cows had only spent a day or two grazing in a pasture–Pappy let them out of their stalls after milking. As the cows walked from their stalls in the direction of the barn door, they defecated all over the barn floor.

When I observed slippery manure everywhere, it prompted me to try a new way of entertaining myself; I grabbed hold of a cow's tail while she pulled me behind her. The slippery manure made it possible for me to slide across the barn's floor with ease. Unfortunately, one of the cows that I grabbed by the tail didn't appreciate my doing so and began running as fast as she could towards the barn door. However, rather than let go of her tail, I held on with both hands and enjoyed the ride. Unfortunately, I somehow lost my balance and fell headfirst into a concrete gutter that was filled with soupy cow manure, hitting the hard surface with sufficient force to knock me out.

As soon as Pappy noticed that I wasn't getting up, he ran over to the location where I was lying, grabbed hold of me with both hands and pulled me from the manure-filled gutter. Quickly realizing that I was unconscious, Pappy then brought me to a nearby faucet and ran water over my head until I regained consciousness. After making sure that I was physically alright, he gently put me down. Then he began telling me in the strongest terms possible that I was never again to grab hold of a cow's tail for the purpose of sliding across the barn floor. Due to the unpleasant experience I'd just had, I followed Pappy's orders to the letter.

Another time I disturbed an angry gander while walking past the barn and was promptly attacked. That is to say the gander folded his two feathered wings out in such a way as to make himself appear larger than life and charged at me. The gander's aggressive gesture worked in that I felt nearly scared to death by his intimidating presence. The animal hissed and darted his orange colored beak at my face. The angry gander was undoubtedly protecting his territory, but I perceived his actions as an unprovoked attack by a vicious animal! In a nervous reaction, I grabbed hold of his neck with both of my hands and held on for dear life! I continued holding onto the gander by the neck until my brother Freddie heard a lot of commotion and ran over to the area and rescued me from my precarious, albeit humorous situation.

Pappy's 527 acres of land consisted of four adjacent farms that he had purchased years prior to my birth. Those farms were: the home place (described above), the Olson place, the Call place, and the Stoddie place. Closest to Pappy's farm was the Olson place, and on that farm was an old abandoned 1947 Chrysler Windsor to be specific. Pappy parked it there after he purchased the Bel Air. I loved hopping inside that rusted-out old vehicle when I was a boy and pretend I was driving around the Olson place.

The next closest farm was the Call place, and to get there I had to walk a good distance past the Olson place on Rindahl Valley Road. Along the way, there was a curve in the road where a grove of trees stood. Those trees created a shaded area that stretched across the road at certain times of the day. My brother Jeff gave me rides on his bike past that stretch of road from time to time. One day, as I felt the cool shade of those trees cover us, I shouted to him, "Holy Christ Jeff, we should call this place Shady Lane!" Well, the name stuck and from that point on Jeff and I referred to that curve in the road on the way to the Call place as Shady Lane.

Just past Shady Lane was the Call place, and on that farm was a steep hill with a small plateau on top. There was also a water pump on the Call place that Pappy used to provide water for livestock. Beside that pump was a large water tank made from concrete and stone. What I remember most clearly about the water tank is that there was always a variety of frogs or toads of different colors swimming in and around the tank. There was also a number of dead mice floating about in the water. They had undoubtedly fallen in the tank while attempting to take a drink of water, and unable to crawl back out again, eventually drowned in the water. Beside the pump was a shed with an open window frame in the wall.

The fourth farm was called the Stoddie place. My favorite memory of the Stoddie place has to do with a mysterious apple tree that produced the best tasting apples that I've ever enjoyed throughout my entire life. Whether accurate or not I do not know, but one of my sisters told me the "wild" apple tree on the Stoddie place produced a kind of fruit that could not be found anywhere else in the world. That story may well be little more than Severson family folklore. However, the fact remains that I've never enjoyed a better-tasting apple anywhere that I have lived than the ones produced on that tree. Another fact that remains is that I've never seen that type of apple in any grocery store or farmers market in any city where I've lived. So, if the tree didn't produce one-of-a-kind apples, it certainly produced extremely rare apples.

Suddenly, my thoughts returned to the present. As I glanced around at the ruins that were once the handsome red barn of my youth, it occurred to me that two generations of Severson families had tended herds of productive dairy cows inside that barn. However, a third generation of Seversons would never have the privilege of doing so. As I stood in front of what was once my father's well-maintained dairy farm, it occurred to me that more than my brother Larry had passed away–our father's dairy farm was gone as well. In truth, an entire way of life had passed with Larry's death. Whatever happens to the land in the future, I thought to myself, it will never again be a Severson family farm. With that sober realization, I stepped inside my car and drove down the poorly-maintained driveway for what I reasonably believe was the last time.

INNOCENCE LOST

When I was a young child, my world consisted of what was located on Pappy's farm. However, there was an outside world that I visited from time to time. Our closest neighbors on the farm were Inga and George Slyfield, a retired couple who spent their summer months in Wisconsin, but spent their winter months in Florida. Their house was on Telemarken Road, slightly to the south of Pappy's driveway. Inga was a grade school teacher and George taught junior high as well as high school. As a child, I thought it was kind of strange that George and Inga weren't dairy farmers. Also, not knowing what Florida was, I thought it even stranger that they left for that place every winter. In spite of those two perceived eccentricities, I remember the Slyfields as very nice people.

For Halloween, my sister Deloris and I used to go trick-or-treating at the Slyfield's home. In fact, their house was the only place we went trick-or-treating as children. I didn't wear a Halloween costume though. Instead, I smeared charcoal on my face and walked over to their hose in pursuit of candy or some other treat. What Deloris and I usually received was an apple or orange and perhaps a popcorn ball. I don't recall them ever giving us candy. George passed away when he was 94 years old in 1994, and Inga passed away at 101 years of age in 2006. They are buried at the South Beef River Lutheran Cemetery.

To the south of the Slyfield home on Telemarken Road was a location that our family referred to as over the hill. However, most people in the area euphemistically referred to the stretch of road as purgatory. It came to be called purgatory due to the fact that the poorly-maintained gravel road frequently washed out after heavy rainstorms, and those washouts made it seem as though it took forever to pass through the area via automobile. At the end of Telemarken Road, or on the other side of purgatory, were two farms that are of considerable importance to my family. Specifically, the Hanson and Holen dairy farms where my maternal ancestors settled after immigrating to the United States.

The first of my ancestors to arrive in the United States were my great-great-grandparents, Hans Høyeson and Thone Stenserdatter, who immigrated to America in 1852. Accompanying them on their long and arduous voyage was my great-grandfather Henry Hanson, who was an eight-year-old boy. Great-grandfather Henry enlisted in the Union Army during the Civil War. When his enlistment ended, he returned to Wisconsin and eventually married my great-grandmother, Gunhild Thompson. He later purchased an 80-acre farm from the railroad in the Beaver Creek area of Jackson County, Wisconsin, and took up farming as his occupation. My grandfather Martin H. Hanson, and my mother Helen Margaret Hanson, were both born on that same farm.

The more distant of the two homesteads located on the other side of purgatory was the dairy farm where my great-grandparents Gilbert and Kaja Holen lived. Gilbert immigrated to the United States in 1872. After establishing himself financially and purchasing the Holen farm, he married my great-grandmother, Kaja Olson. My grandma Olena G. Holen was born on Gilbert and Kaja's dairy farm. When great-grandfather Henry Hanson passed away, grandpa Martin took over operation of the 80 acre farm. Approximately eight years later, he married his neighbor, Olena G. Holen, who lived on the adjacent dairy farm. My mother, Helen, was later born there in 1916.

Returning now to the present, I momentarily contemplated driving past the Hanson and Holen farms. However, I reluctantly decided there was insufficient time. Instead, I decided to return to Osseo. I drove north until Telemarken Road intersected with Rindahl Valley Road. The next closest farm to Pappy's place after the Slyfields was the home of Leonard and Agnes Rindahl. They lived at the eastern end of Rindahl Valley Road, which is the same gravel road that leads to the Call place. Although Leonard had been a dairy farmer most of his life, he also worked at the Uniroyal tire company in Eau Claire. His wife Agnes had worked at the Osseo Area Nursing Home and Hospital as the manager of the laundry department. What came to mind as I glanced in the direction of the Rindahl family farm was their granddaughter Sandy. Sweet Sandy was my age and my first sweetheart.

As I continued my drive towards County Road B, I remembered how Sandy was as cute as a girl could be and that I enjoyed visiting the Rindahl farm with Ma when I was little just so I could spend some time with her. We attended Sunday school classes together at South Beef River Lutheran Church, and it was usually after the worship service that we stopped by their farm for a visit. We played together and I loved every minute of the time I spent in her company. Sandy's grandpa Leonard passed away at 71 years of age in 1978, and her grandma Agnes passed away at 84 years of age in 1998. They are buried at the South Beef River Lutheran Cemetery where so many of my early childhood neighbors, friends and family members are located.

About the same distance from Pappy's farm as Leonard and Agnes Rindahl's farm, but going in a westerly direction on Rindahl Valley Road, was another elderly couple named Carrie and Kalmer Rindahl. Incidentally, Kalmer and Leonard Rindahl were two of Inga Slyfield's brothers. Kalmer and Carrie were hardworking dairy farmers their entire lives. As with virtually all of the neighbors in the area, Kalmer and Carrie's children had grown and moved away before I was old enough to get to know them. About halfway between the two farms stood a place known as the three oaks. Carrie and Ma visited each other several times over the years and whenever their visits ended, one person walked the other halfway home, or as far as the three oaks. Carrie Rindahl was Ma's best friend, and I'm certain that Ma was Carrie's best friend as well. Kalmer passed away at 95 years of age in 1986, and Carrie passed away at 76 years of age in 1975. They are buried beside one another at the South Beef River Lutheran Cemetery. My sister Virginia and her husband Wayne later purchased their farm.

Beyond Carrie and Kalmer's farm lived a bachelor named Kermit

Pederson. His farm was located directly behind Carrie and Kalmer's, but on South Prairie Road rather than Rindahl Valley Road. As with nearly everyone else in the valley, Kermit was already elderly by the time I was born. However, he remained actively engaged in farming. My fondest memories of Kermit are that he was about as kind as a gentleman could be. However, even as a child I couldn't help but notice that once Pappy stopped to visit with him, it seemed as though their conversations went on forever. I assumed that as a bachelor, Kermit didn't have that many people to talk to, so whenever the opportunity to visit arose, he was not going to let the moment end quickly. Nevertheless, I tend to remember him as a kindly, albeit long-winded gentleman. Kermit Pederson was Pappy's best friend, and I'm reasonably certain Pappy was his best friend as well. Kermit Pederson passed away at 70 years of age in 1981 and was buried at the South Beef River Lutheran Cemetery. Gary Severson–my brother Larry's oldest son–purchased the farm shortly after Kermit's death.

Further down the road and thus farther removed from my world lived another elderly couple named John and Alice Martin. I remember very little about John except that he and Alice were kind and friendly people. John and Alice operated a truck farm business. That is to say, they planted, harvested and sold a variety of fresh vegetables and fruits to individuals and area markets. I can't say that I remember them stopping by our farm for social visits, but I do recall Alice stopping to sell Ma fresh fruits and vegetables. As was Ma's way, she always agreed to buy a few items. John passed away at 87 years of age in 1974, and Alice passed away at 87 years of age in 1999. They are buried at West Lawn Cemetery in Augusta.

The only other person that I remember living near Pappy's farm was an elderly widow named Clara Edwards. Clara's deceased husband was Harvey Hilton Edwards, but I never met him. What I remember about Clara is that she was poor–extremely poor. Well, that and the fact that she wore thick eyeglasses that made her look something like the cartoon character Mr. Magoo. Harvey Edwards passed away at 70 years of age in 1965. He is buried at the Levis Cemetery. Clara passed away at 76 years of age in 1977, and is buried beside him at the Levis Cemetery.

After leaving Rindahl Valley Road and returning to the paved County Road B, I decided to turn right, or east, to a location that I loved as a child. Specifically, the Levis Store, an old-fashioned country store that was owned by a Swedish American couple named Grace and Leonard Person. Leonard was good friends with Pappy, and I loved listing to their conversations when I was a child. The Levis Store stocked hardware items, farm-related products, some clothing items and a few groceries. However, what I remember most about the place is that they always had ice-cold pop and a variety of delicious candies for sale. Whenever I went to the Levis Store it was always with Ma and Pappy, Ma always purchased a Slo-Poke or a Sugar Daddy for me to enjoy while she enjoyed a Nut Goodie. Pappy never purchased any candy. Leonard and Grace retired in 1975, and sold their business to a couple named Richard and Dorothy Otto. Today, the place is called the Levis Lodge, and is essentially a bar.

Good neighbors make good friends
Norwegian Proverb

As I continued my drive back towards the City of Osseo, I passed two more gravel roads that were of great importance to the Severson family; roads where my paternal great-grandfather Sever Siem and great-grandmother Marit Hansdatter Hattrem settled shortly after emigrating from Norway to the United States in 1882, and the road where my other paternal great-grandparents, Kari Christensdatter Mork and Ole Johannesen Odlorønningen, owned an 80-acre dairy farm. Incidentally, the farm owned by great-grandfather Sever Siem was purchased by my brother Larry in 1968.

Another 80-acre dairy farm located in the same area was purchased by my grandfather Sigurd Severson when he was a young man, and he continued farming there for several years. My father, Norman Henry Severson, was born on that farm. Several years later, when Pappy was a young man, he purchased that same dairy farm. Not long after that, he married Ma, and they continued farming there until after my oldest two sisters, Margaret and Dorothy, were born. Before Larry was born, though, Pappy sold that property and purchased the farm located on Telemarken Road, which is the farm where I lived for the first seven years of my life.

A few miles from Pappy's farm stood the South Beef River Lutheran Church. Although I've never been a religious person, I've always felt a strong connection with the church, and to this day I think of it as one of the most beautiful buildings I have ever seen. For me, the church represents, in the most favorable way possible, the proud heritage of the farming community that I was a part of as a child, a world that was overwhelmingly Lutheran in faith and Norwegian in ancestry. It didn't hurt that the vast majority of the people who were members of the congregation at South Beef River were hardworking dairy farmers either.

I have always been of the opinion that the South Beef River Lutheran Church is a magnificent building to observe, both inside and outside. The altar baptismal font, communion rail and pulpit are constructed of richly grained oak, as are the pews, balcony and the stained glass lancet window frames. The oak floors throughout the sanctuary have a slightly darker stain than the previously mentioned woodwork. Behind the altar is an impressive painting of a redeemed sinner rising towards Heaven where the Lord Jesus Christ waits to receive him in glorious splendor. The stained glass lancet windows display a variety of intricately detailed images of Christian and Lutheran significance. Although the building is beautiful to look at both inside and out, I can not honestly say I enjoyed attending the worship services or going to Sunday school very much. Fortunately, I only sporadically attended Sunday School classes and worship services at the South Beef River Lutheran Church when I was a child.

As I approached the church from County Highway B, I looked up at the majestic church steeple and decided to stop and park beside the building for a while. As I sat inside my car, I was reminded that my brother Larry's funeral was going to take place inside the church the following day. As I sat and contemplated that depressing thought, I was reminded of just how beautiful the sanctuary inside the church is, that when the sunlight shines through the stained glass windows at a certain angle it creates a peaceful, almost ethereal kind of ambiance. As my thoughts wandered, I gradually drifted back in time to the year 1966, when my life was still filled with innocence and wonder.

About six miles northwest of the South Beef River Lutheran Church was the rest of my world: the City of Osseo of Osseo, a thriving farm community of approximately 1,144 residents. Osseo was also the cultural center of the surrounding community. Farmers from several miles away did most of their socializing, grocery shopping, banking and business in the City of Osseo. They also sent their kids to school there. My oldest siblings attended various country schools including the Levis School and the Church View School. However, all of the country schools that my older siblings attended had closed before I started attending the first grade in 1965.

Over the years, Pappy bought, sold and upgraded his farm equipment to the point where he owned an extensive inventory of modern farm equipment. The farm machinery included four tractors: a Farmall H, a Farmall M, an International 460 and a Cockshutt Model 50 Deluxe. My favorite tractor among the four was the Cockshutt, which I always referred to as the Mighty Cockshutt. The Cockshutt Model 50 Deluxe was a strong and handsome tractor that could do everything Pappy asked of it and then some. The tractor was colorfully painted harvest yellow with bright red trim. Also, unlike most tractors of the day, the Cockshutt had wide front tires which provided greater stability when maneuvering about. It also had what were considered enormous rear tires for the day. Framing those massive tires were two red fenders that protected the operator from danger.

Pappy used the Cockshutt for the heaviest work such as plowing and disking the fields, baling hay, chopping corn and pulling the combine used to harvest oats. Its powerful Buda six-cylinder engine, rated at 52 horsepower, gave off a unique screaming sound that was unlike any other tractor I've ever heard. Cockshutt farm implements are no longer sold today, and they were probably never a dominant name in the field of agriculture throughout the United States. However, his brother Lawrence sold Cockshutt farm machinery for a living. So, Pappy purchased his farm equipment from him whenever possible.

The time I spent on Pappy's farm from the time of my birth through 1966 was a golden age of innocence, play and carefree adventure. I was much too young to experience any of the difficult, backbreaking labor that my older siblings faced every day of the year. Unlike my older siblings, I had never milked a cow nor driven a tractor at that time. Nor did I take part in harvesting the endless fields of crops that my older siblings had experienced. I was given simple chores such as curry combing the dairy cows and picking up the leftover twine after untold bales of hay had been fed to them. I sometimes carried a little firewood inside the farmhouse and occasionally scraped manure from the barn floor into the gutters as well. However, I hadn't engaged in any of the demanding type of physical labor that my older brothers and sisters experienced nearly every day.

My older siblings had experienced some lean financial times as well. However, by the time I was born, those times had all but disappeared. There was still an endless amount of work for my older siblings to complete each day, and most of the chores involved intensive manual labor. However, through hard work and sound financial management, Pappy had become a highly successful farmer by 1966. Over time he carefully developed the sandy soil found throughout his farm to the fullest extent possible, and his land produced bountiful yields of crops every year. More importantly, everything he owned, including the land, the livestock and the machinery was paid for. In other words, Pappy was completely debt free as the summer of 1966 arrived.

As previously stated, my childhood was essentially a carefree time of unlimited play and adventure, and that was the way my day began on June 22, 1966. The heat was already quite intense as I broke from the hurried kitchen scene where Ma had been serving breakfast. As she did every morning, Ma made sure that everyone in the family received a hearty breakfast to start their day. Her breakfasts usually consisted of boiled, fried or scrambled eggs, bacon, pancakes and toast. There was milk or Kool-Aid for the kids to drink and coffee for the adults, always a lot of coffee!

After eating breakfast that morning, I stepped away from the table and went outside through the front screen door onto the concrete steps that sat at the front door to the farmhouse. As I had undoubtedly done the previous morning and the morning before that, I darted around to the side of the building. Once there I found what I was looking for, my collection of toys. By any measure, I had a lot of toys. There were toy tractors, wagons, trucks and other items that I played with virtually every day. They were top-quality metal toys too, not the plastic kind that children received in subsequent generations. My yellow Tonka truck and crane were two of my favorites. I turned seven one month earlier and toys were still a big part of my world.

Shortly after I began what might have been the imaginary building of a new bridge over a mighty, raging river or a huge tunnel stretching for several miles beneath the mountains above, I was visited by my 11 year old brother Jeff. He had finished his breakfast by then and walked outside to join me for a few minutes before heading out to the field to bale hay with our older sister Gloria and Pappy. I had just turned seven and Jeff was 11 going on 20. Prior to my so much as getting out of bed that morning, Jeff had been awake long enough to have finished his multiple chores around the farm which would have included tending to his calves and other livestock as well as assisting Pappy with milking the dairy cows.

Soon after Jeff arrived, Pappy and Gloria exited the farmhouse and that meant it was time for the three of them to go to work. As they departed for the field that day, I once again found myself alone at play, but that was all right with me. I almost always played alone and was content to do so again that day. Almost immediately, I once again escaped into the fantasy world of a seven-year-old boy at play. I scarcely watched as the three drove down our driveway onto Telemarken Road and down Rindahl Valley Road past Shady Lane to the Call place and eventually to the field on top of a plateau where they were going to be baling hay that day.

I can't exactly remember the image of them leaving that day. That is to say, I don't remember what time it was or who was sitting where or what vehicles they were operating as they left to bale hay. However, I remember they were all home and then they were no longer at home. As I've told myself many times over the years that followed, I have to remember their departure that day. It was June 22, 1966, and it was the last time that I would see my father alive. Later that hot, summer day, Pappy's life would be unjustly crushed from him with unmerciful brutality and great violence.

My time at play passed leisurely along that morning. The mighty bridge or underground tunnel that I had pretended to construct was either finished or I had grown bored with whatever it was that I had pretended to do. At some point my nine-year-old sister Deloris and I found ourselves on the Call place. The Call place is less than one mile from the home place and my sister and I may have walked there at some point or hitched a ride. However, truth be told, I don't really remember how we arrived there to that day. Nevertheless, the two of us eventually found ourselves playing inside an old shed by the water pump while Pappy, Gloria and Jeff were hard at work baling hay in the previously mentioned field at the top of the plateau.

The only way to get to the top of the plateau to bale the field of hay that had grown there was to drive the necessary farm equipment up a gradually sloping hillside. The farm equipment used to bale the hay included the Cockshutt Model 50 Deluxe, which pulled both the hay baler and a hay wagon that was hitched to the back of the baler. A smaller Farmall H tractor was also used to haul the loads of freshly baled hay from the plateau to the home place where it would later be stacked inside Pappy's hay barn. When Pappy, Gloria and Jeff finally finished baling the field of hay on top of the plateau, it was time for them to drive all of the equipment back down the sloping hillside. Pappy Instructed Jeff to drive the Cockshutt and hay baler down the hillside. Then Pappy jumped on the Farmall H and began hauling a load of hay home. Gloria elected to ride with Jeff on the Cockshutt. Jeff and Gloria followed immediately behind Pappy as everyone departed the plateau.

At some point while Pappy was pulling the load of hay down the gradually sloping hillside, the wagon rushed forward towards the Farmall H, causing it to tip over. Sadly, when the Farmall H tipped over it landed directly on top of Pappy and instantly crushed him to death. Unfortunately, Jeff and Gloria both witnessed the horrific event unfold. Almost immediately, Jeff stopped the Cockshutt as Gloria jumped off the tractor and ran over to Pappy. Upon arrival, she found Pappy lying unconscious. Without hesitation, Gloria immediately ran over to the nearby Rindahl farm where she called for an ambulance. As soon as Jeff turned the Cockshutt off he also ran over to the scene of the accident. There Jeff found his father laying unconscious, with a stream of blood trickling from his mouth. Not exactly sure what to do, Jeff initially took off in the direction of the Rindahl farm. Then, the 11-year-old boy paused for a moment while he kneeled and prayed to God to let his father live. Then he resumed running from the field. Jeff later lamented that in spite of his heartfelt prayer, he intuitively understood his father was dead.

I was unaware of anything out of the ordinary having happened until I saw my sister Gloria come running past the shed. She was running as fast as the wind and it was obvious to me that she was running with a purpose. Gloria quickly ran past us without noticing that Deloris and

I were in the shed. She ran all the way to Agnes Rindahl's house so that she could call an ambulance. We didn't have a telephone at our house as Pappy didn't believe in such things. However, Gloria knew that Agnes Rindahl had a telephone, and she had the presence of mind to run there to make the telephone call.

A while after Gloria ran past us, Deloris and I observed our brother Jeff running by the shed in the same direction. I noticed he had the same serious determination on his face that Gloria had expressed when she ran by us sometime before. However, unlike Gloria, Jeff noticed us inside the shed and stopped to face us. He was standing outside looking in while Deloris and I were standing inside the shed looking out. Suddenly, Jeff yelled at us with panic visible on his suddenly boyish face, "The tractor tipped over on Dad!" I saw that he was visibly shaken as I watched him through the open window. Then, as quickly as he appeared, Jeff took off running in the same direction that Gloria had previously ran. Suddenly, Jeff stopped and shouted back at us, "You kids better get the hell home right away!"

We did exactly as we were told and left the shed where we had been playing. As Deloris and I were walking down Rindahl Valley Road towards the home place, shortly after we passed through Shady Lane, a silver colored station wagon that served as Osseo's ambulance sped past us on its way to the field where the accident happened. The two of us watched it pass by with its makeshift red light flashing on top. As I watched the vehicle pass by, I wanted to hurry home to be with Ma. I was certain that everything would be all right if I could just be in her presence.

Before Deloris and I had walked any farther than the Olson place, the ambulance rushed past us again en route to the hospital in Osseo. As the vehicle rushed by, Deloris and I observed a blood-stained cloth covering a body that was in the back of the ambulance. I naturally assumed the body was that of our injured father. Several years later it was explained to me that the station wagon which served as Osseo's ambulance was owned by a gentleman named Reider Oftedahl, who was also the local undertaker. He rigged the station wagon in such a way that it firmly held an elevated stretcher in place whenever he transported an injured individual needing medical attention from the location of an accident to the closest hospital. It was the way that Mr. Oftedahl had modified the vehicle that allowed my sister and me to observe the body in the back of the ambulance as it passed us by.

Eventually, my sister Deloris and I finished our walk home. When we arrived I was certain that Ma would hold me and make everything better. However, as we approached the front yard, that was not how things unfolded. Quite unexpectedly, we observed Ma walking from the house with the assistance of the aluminum walker she had recently started using when ambulating about. She was slowly walking in the direction of an unknown car that was parked in front of the woodshed. A stranger slowly walked beside her. It was clear that Ma had been crying as her eyes were red and swollen.

When Ma saw us, she briefly acknowledged our presence. However, visibly shaken, all she could do was mumble something like, "I'll be home as soon as I can kids." Then she turned towards the stranger as he carefully opened the passenger door of his car for her. Without uttering another word, Ma slowly entered the car and rode away with him. A cloud of dust rose behind the car as it quickly sped off down the dirt driveway from Pappy's farm. I would later learn that the stranger driving Ma away that day was Doctor Brad Garber. He was taking Ma to the hospital in Osseo to identify Pappy's lifeless body.

Later that day, several people arrived at our farm to visit with and give comfort to Ma. Others stopped by to help with the chores. I vividly remember seeing our neighbor Jimmy Rindahl in the barn. He arrived to help 11-year-old Jeff milk the cows that evening. When I saw him in the barn I walked up to him and asked, "Why are you here milking the cows Jimmy?" He kindly smiled back at me but refrained from answering my question. Instead, Jimmy turned and looked the other way. As Jimmy rested his head against the cow that he was milking, he said, in a voice that cracked with emotion, "I don't know, Danny, I guess I just wanted to help with the chores today."

Another person who visited the farm that day was my best friend and nephew, Brian Maug. As kids will often do, we began playing with some of the other kids who had also arrived. Brian's younger brother Doug was there as well. At one point Brian said his younger brother had started laughing when his parents told him his grandpa had been killed in a tractor accident earlier that day. When I heard Brian utter those words I remember freezing up for a moment, unable to process what it was that Brian had just said to me. In hindsight, I realize Brian was explaining his little brother's peculiar reaction to the unfortunate news he had heard, and did so based on the assumption that I knew that Pappy had been killed earlier in the day.

However, the truth of the matter is I had no idea that Pappy had been killed in the accident earlier that day and I remember being absolutely astonished at Brian's words. It struck me as outlandish and ridiculous for him to have said such a thing. You see, in all the chaos of the day, nobody had taken the time to explain to me that my father was killed in the tractor accident that happened earlier in the day. "Pappy ain't dead!" I shouted at Brian. However, Brian didn't back down and said once again that his grandpa had died. We argued about the matter for a moment or two more before Brian said, "Go and ask grandma if you don't believe me, Dan, grandpa got killed today."

I didn't believe Brian. I didn't believe a goddamn word of what he was saying. You see, in the mind of a small boy, a seven-year-old boy to be specific, the obvious is not always so obvious. I knew that Pappy had been in a tractor accident earlier in the day and that he had been taken away in an ambulance. I also remembered seeing a blood-stained cloth covering his body as the ambulance passed by my sister Deloris and me. And I remembered seeing Ma in tears as she briefly departed Pappy's farm in a stranger's vehicle. However, in spite of being aware of all of those things, it never occurred to me that Pappy had been killed. It just didn't seem possible. I was so certain that Brian was wrong I took him up on his challenge and walked inside the farmhouse to discuss the matter with Ma.

As if only yesterday, I remember walking inside the farmhouse and approaching Ma in a matter-of-fact manner to ask her about Brian's outrageous comment. I found her sitting at the kitchen table with some adults drinking coffee. I leaned up close to her ear and asked, "Ma, did Pappy die today?" In a distant, monotone kind of voice she mumbled something like, "Ya Danny, Pappy died today." Then, she gently pushed me away and slowly turned to resume her conversation with the adults at the table. As an adult, I fully understand how Ma was undoubtedly overwhelmed by everything that had happened and was quite possibly in shock. However, as a seven-year-old boy, I was enraged by what had just happened. In that vulnerable moment, there was nothing in the world that I needed so much as to be held by my mother. However, rather than hold me, she pushed me away. That painfully difficult moment was the end of my innocence.

Later that night, I grew tired and eventually made my way to my bed. I walked past the people in the kitchen and crawled into bed for the night. I remember lying in bed that evening and looking out of the bedroom window at the moonlight, watching the shadows of various tree branches as they moved slowly across the bedroom walls. As I watched the shadows of those tree branches swaying about, I thought about Pappy. With the limited knowledge of life and death that I had as a seven-year-old boy, I wondered what it felt like to be killed, to be crushed to death under the weight of a tractor. In time my curiosity and sadness were supplanted by an overwhelming sense of anger and outrage. Still later, I drifted off into the troubled, restless sleep of an angry young boy.

Remember tonight...for it is the beginning of always
Dante Alighieri

Pappy's wake was held a couple of days later at the funeral home in Osseo, and I can remember the event as if it happened only yesterday. Most of my family was present. However, Freddie had not yet made it back from Camp Pendleton, California, where he was stationed with the United States Marine Corps. Those of us who were present walked in solemn procession past Pappy's casket as he lay in repose. Not really sure what was expected of me, I attempted to mimic the behavior of my older siblings as they walked past the casket in solemn procession.

As I passed by the open casket, I stopped for a moment and gazed at Pappy as he "slept" in his handsome casket of richly grained wood. Much to my surprise, Pappy was wearing a suit and tie. How strange, I thought to myself, that Pappy was dressed that way. Not once in my life had I seen him wearing anything but striped overalls. Later in life I would see photographs of Pappy wearing a suit and tie, but I had not yet seen him in such out-of-character clothing, and I remember telling myself that it looked very strange. At one point I casually reached my hand out and touched his arm. His lifeless limb felt as hard as a rock. His arm felt as hard as my angry young heart.

Pappy's funeral was held at the South Beef River Lutheran Church on June 25, 1966. I remember attending the funeral, but I can't recall any of the words that were spoken. What I do remember is how full the small country church appeared to me to be. In preparation for the funeral, Ma purchased a new outfit for me to wear that included a dark blue jacket with a handsome red vest and clip-on tie. She also purchased a new white shirt and dress shoes for me to wear. At the beginning of the funeral, my siblings and I were all escorted to the front pews that are reserved for immediate family members. As the youngest, I was seated to Ma's left and my sister Deloris was seated to her immediate right, followed by the other siblings.

While being escorted to the pews, I also remember seeing a man that I did not recognize there with us. He was a very handsome man I said to myself, with well-groomed hair and what passed for a respectable suit. Not knowing who that young man was fueled my curiosity. So, after we were all seated, I eventually turned to Ma and said, "Ma, who is that man sitting at the end of the pew?" As I asked the question I pointed my finger directly at him so Ma would know who it was that I was asking about. Ma looked at the man and then back at me. As Ma did so she leaned down towards me and whispered to me in a matter-of-fact voice, "Why, for crying out loud, Danny, that's your brother Larry!" I was astonished by what she said. Larry looked so different in his suit, clean shaven face and well-groomed hair that I didn't even recognize him as my oldest brother!

I must have spent an hour or more in the parking lot of the South Beef River Lutheran Church, contemplating Larry's funeral the following day, and reminiscing about Pappy's funeral held many years before. After taking one last look at the church, I started my car and took off in the direction of Osseo, knowing there were several other places of personal importance that I wanted to visit before the day ended. The first place that I decided to go was the house where I lived from 1967 through 1977, when I graduated from high school. When I arrived at the corner of Francis Street and US Highway 10, I parked my car and gazed out at the house where I had lived. The house had been bought and sold several times since I lived there, and it had been remodeled as well. However, as I stepped from my car, I watched peacefully as the unfamiliar house slowly transformed its appearance to that of the home I remembered as Ma's place.

MA'S PLACE

In what seemed like a very short time, but was actually around 10 months, my brother Larry took over the operation of Pappy's farm and Ma moved us into a house she purchased in Osseo, a community of 1,144 people at the time. Although the community was located a little more than 10 miles from Pappy's farm and I had visited there several times, moving from the farm to the City of Osseo was a real shock to the system. First and foremost among the many changes that I experienced was the seemingly unending noise.

Our house was located at the intersection of Francis Street and US Highway 10, and the "roar" of so many cars and trucks passing by at all hours of the day and night was unsettling. It took several weeks before I was able to fall asleep at night. The nights on Pappy's farm were always quiet and peaceful. The other change that took time to adjust to was the light from streetlights and headlights that shone in my bedroom after sundown. I was used to natural darkness at night, and it was difficult falling asleep with so much artificial light shining in the bedroom at night.

The history books tell us that Osseo was originally founded (surveyed and plotted) in 1857 and incorporated as a village as far back as 1893. However, Osseo wasn't officially named a city until 1941. Later in life, when I researched the history of my family in furtherance of my interest in genealogy, I thought it was compelling that the community was founded around the same period in American history that most of my Norwegian ancestors immigrated to the United States.

One of the things the history books don't adequately explain is how the community's earliest settlers decided on the admittedly unusual name of Osseo. That said, it is known that a famous writer named Henry Wadsworth Longfellow published his poem, "The Song Of Hiawatha," in 1856, and it has been speculated that one or more of Osseo's original settlers gave the community its name after reading that poem. Here is the stanza from that epic poem which references a man named Osseo:

> This with joy beheld Iagoo
> And he said in haste: "Behold it!
> See the sacred Star of Evening!
> You shall hear a tale of wonder,
> Hear the story of Osseo,
> Son of the Evening Star, Osseo!

The house we moved to was located at 313 Francis Street. However, at some point after I moved away from Osseo, the address changed to 13402 10th Street. I felt a familial connection to the house right away since it had been built by my grandpa Sigurd Severson. He purchased the land where the house was built in 1945 but didn't finish building it until 1948. Of course, grandpa Sigurd had sold the property to another family years before Ma purchased the place. She purchased the house from a gentleman named Frank Warnke in 1967, and we moved into the home a few days before my eighth birthday.

Right from the start, I began referring to the new home as Ma's place. My brother Irvin and my two sisters Gloria and Deloris moved into the house along with Ma and me. However, my brother Jeff didn't move to Osseo with the rest of us, choosing instead to stay on Pappy's farm with our older brother Larry and his family. Of course, Jeff was far too young to be permanently separated from his mother, and about one year later, he moved to Osseo to be with the rest of his family. I remember my move as if it happened yesterday. I got on the school bus at Pappy's farm the same as always that day. However, when the school day ended, I didn't get back on the bus for the return trip to Pappy's farm. Instead, I walked to my new home in the house that Ma purchased in the City of Osseo.

Our new house was truly modern compared with the farmhouse. For one thing, it had a thermostat for controlled central heating, whereas the farmhouse had a wood-burning stove. Later that year, Ma had air conditioning installed, so we were physically comfortable throughout the year. Directly beside Ma's place was my sister Margaret's home. At the time of the move to Osseo, Ma's condition had worsened to where she was essentially confined to a wheelchair. With her health in serious decline from rheumatoid arthritis, Ma found it comforting to know that her oldest daughter was nearby in case of an emergency.

From my perspective as an eight-year-old boy, having our two homes located next to each other meant one thing: having kids to play with whenever I wanted. At various times throughout my youth, I was best friends with each of the Keffer kids: Paul, Donald and Joseph. Over time our households became so intertwined that we casually walked in and out of each other's homes as if we lived there. That is to say, we did not knock before entering as a visitor ordinarily does. We just walked in and began interacting with the other members of the home. We didn't sit down at the table with the members of the other family at mealtime, but we thought nothing of staying at their home until the family was finished eating so that we could resume doing whatever it was that we were doing when someone put the food on the table and told that household's family members it was time to eat.

The yard around Ma's place was larger than the one on Pappy's farm, and it was a lot prettier too. The grass was always well-maintained by my older siblings. In truth, I never mowed the grass at Ma's place until my older siblings had moved away. There were several mature trees throughout the yard, including two good-sized Colorado blue spruce trees. For the first few years after the move to Osseo, my brother Jeff attached colorful Christmas lights to those two attractive trees. The colored lights looked particularly spectacular after a fresh blanket of snow had fallen on their branches.

Next to the house was a one-car detached garage and inside the garage was a large wooden workbench that I used countless times throughout the years I lived in Osseo. The attic located above the garage was full of scrap lumber when we moved to Osseo, and I took full advantage of the cache of unexpected materials to build a variety of items. I used some of the lumber to construct a six-foot-long wooden go-kart that I painted silver in color. Initially, I used wooden axles and the wheels fell off every time I tried to ride it. However, after I attached a couple of steel axles to the bottom it worked fairly well. That said, I had a lot more fun building the go-kart than I did riding it around.

I was given a set of boxing gloves as my Christmas present the first year that we lived at Ma's place. Not long after that my friends and I began holding boxing matches inside the garage. Ma gave me a 110 pound weightlifting set for Christmas the next year and shortly after that my friend Cary Hagen and I started a weight lifting club inside the garage. At different times there were several of us who worked out together lifting weights. In time though, our collective interest in weightlifting was supplanted by some other kind of activity, and as that happened the weightlifting club unceremoniously disbanded.

I also raised rabbits inside the garage, but only for a brief time. The problem with the way I raised rabbits was that I allowed them to run freely about inside the garage. Soon there was rabbit excrement everywhere, and when Ma learned of the situation, I was ordered to clean up the mess and give the rabbits away. I also kept a guinea pig and hamster inside the garage–but always inside their cages. The guinea pig died under mysterious circumstances. Ma "suggested" it might have eaten some leftover rabbit food by mistake and choked to death. However, I couldn't help but wonder if someone who wanted that guinea pig to go away placed poison inside the cage. After all, who ever heard of a guinea pig dying from eating rabbit food?

That same summer, my hamster mysteriously escaped from his cage. Ma "suggested" the animal must have squeezed his way through the bars of his cage and run away. However, it always seemed a lot more plausible to me that someone who wanted that hamster to go away opened the door to his cage and let him out. After all, who ever heard of a hamster squeezing through the metal bars on a cage specifically designed for hamsters? What really happened to the guinea pig and hamster I will never know. What I do know is that the unpleasant loss of my rabbits, guinea pig and hamster brought about the end of the rodents as pets chapter of my youth.

Not long after we moved to Osseo, Ma asked four of her sons-in-law, Stan Caucutt, Floyd Maug, Wayne Holte and Wally Moyle, to fix up the basement for her. Without the slightest bit of hesitation, all four men agreed to do so and immediately began the process of installing dark simulated wood grain paneling over the cinder block walls and attaching white tiles on the ceiling. They graciously volunteered their services on weekends and evenings until the project was finished. In hindsight, I came to think of that basement remodeling project as a selfless act of kindness on Ma's part. That was because Ma was never able to enter the basement to see for herself what she had created for her children. Her only notion of what the remodeled basement looked like came from the Polaroid photographs that my siblings and I shared with her.

Objectively speaking, the basement was a dark, damp and surprisingly cold place. Subjectively speaking, it was a really enjoyable place to hang out, either alone or with my friends. Due to the coldness of the basement in wintertime, an oil burner was installed and that provided enough heat to make the place feel relatively comfortable. However, whenever the oil burner was turned off, even for a few minutes, the basement turned cold again. Initially, my older siblings spent a lot of time in the basement hanging out with friends. However, after they moved away the basement essentially became my private domain.

Over the years, I built up a good-sized collection of albums and they provided endless hours of listening entertainment. Unlike most teenagers in those days, I wasn't into the popular bands of the day such as Boston. I was more into the music of Bob Dylan. At some point before I moved into the basement, one of my siblings purchased *Bob Dylan's Greatest Hits Volume I*, and *Bob Dylan's Greatest Hits Volume II.* One day I discovered both recordings and after a single listen I was hooked for life on the words and music of Bob Dylan.

The nasal tone of Bob Dylan's voice was pleasing to my ear, and the powerful, sometimes poignant lyrics were always thought-provoking. Most people only appreciate Bob Dylan because of his moving lyrics. However, I found the sound of his nasal voice every bit as enjoyable, at least initially. As I grew older, I gained a greater appreciation for his consistently brilliant lyrics, and as that happened, the meaning of his songs grew in importance as well, and it wasn't only the sound of his voice that I enjoyed. I began to appreciate his song lyrics for the philosophically complex, beautiful, witty and at times hilariously funny compositions that they are. To a lesser extent, I also enjoyed listening to the underappreciated psychedelic music of Donovan as well as The Beatles.

The interior of the house at Ma's place was inviting and considerably more attractive than the house on Pappy's farm. The dining room and living room area was the most attractive part of the house. There was a faux archway that divided the large room into two halves and I was able to appreciate the architectural beauty of the design even as a boy. Beside the archway on the dining room side was a large set of double windows that allowed sunlight to enter the room during the day and moonlight to enter the room at night. It was from those windows that we enjoyed looking out at the Christmas lights on the Colorado blue spruce trees. The dining room and living room areas were spacious and well lit and they had a warm, inviting ambiance about them that I greatly enjoyed. I felt more at home there than inside any other room at Ma's place except for the basement.

My favorite piece of furniture on Pappy's farm was the oak table in the kitchen that we gathered around at mealtime. At Ma's place the comparable centerpiece was a handsome maple table in the dining room. Some of my best and worst memories of growing up in Osseo occurred at that table. By far my worst memory involves the death of my brother Freddie, who was killed in a car accident on Saturday, August 5, 1967. On that night, I was awakened by cries emanating from the living room. As any kid would do when hearing their Ma crying, I got out of bed and walked into the living room to see what was the matter. There in the dark of the night, I found my mother sitting at the table in her wheelchair. She was pounding the curled arthritic fist of her right hand on the table while crying with greater intensity than I'd ever heard her cry before.

Standing there in the darkness with Ma was a one-armed policeman named Harry Strong. Patrolman Strong arrived that night to deliver the news to Ma that her 19-year-old son had been killed in an automobile accident. The single-car crash occurred on State Highway 121 between Pigeon Falls and Northfield. I watched in silence as the one-armed patrolman gently pat Ma on the back with his good arm. As that was what the police officer was doing, I walked over to Ma and did the same. Although we tried our best to comfort her, we both intuitively understood there was no comforting a parent who had just learned her child had been killed in a car accident. Other siblings later arrived at the house and helped comfort Ma. However, in those first few difficult moments, it was only Patrolman Harry Strong and me who stood there in the darkness with her. The two of us watched with a profound sense of sadness as she painfully grieved the loss of her son. I watched my mother as she grew old right before my eyes.

We die only once, and for such a long time
Moliere

Freddie had been living with our brother Larry on what used to be Pappy's farm at the time of his death. Presumably, he was returning home from some unknown location on State Highway 121 when he took a corner too fast for conditions, lost control of his vehicle and went off the road. According to newspaper reports of the event from the Winona Daily News, the car crashed through the barbed wire fence of a farmer named Norman Hegge. When his car left the road, it took out a section of that fence and continued across the front lawn of the Hegge home, jumped the driveway and struck a corner post before coming to a stop. The car traveled approximately 450 feet after it left the highway. Trempealeau County Sheriff Eugene Bijold speculated that Freddie's car struck Mr. Hegge's fence with sufficient force to dislodge a fencepost from the ground, causing it to then sling through the driver-side window of Freddie's car with sufficient force to crush his skull. The County Coroner added that Freddie was killed instantly and that the fatal accident occurred around 9:30p.m.

Ma took the untimely death of her 19-year-old son very hard. I remember her repeatedly crying in the days leading up to the funeral. Then, as if to add insult to her pain and suffering, she received a most unwelcome visit on the day of the funeral from Norman Hegge, the farmer whose fence was admittedly damaged in the car accident. Mr. Hegge appeared at Ma's door and demanded compensation for the damage to his fence. Fortunately, my brother Irvin was present at the time and intervened by reminding Mr. Hegge that Freddie's funeral was scheduled later that day. Irvin further informed Mr. Hegge that if he wanted to discuss compensation for the damage to his property he should consider doing so at a more appropriate time.

As for the funeral itself, I don't remember much about it other than how desperate and vulnerable my mother looked. I also remember noticing how different Freddie's funeral was from Pappy's in terms of the number of people in attendance. There were hardly any people in attendance at Freddie's funeral. For the most part, the only people who attended were members of our immediate family and a few of the people who were Freddie's neighbors when everyone still lived on Pappy's farm. In truth, Freddie never had many friends in life, and few if any of them were in attendance. Even the casket bearers were elderly relatives of Freddie's whom Ma asked to serve in that important role. Finally, I couldn't help but take notice of the fact that due to the severe head trauma Freddie sustained in the automobile accident, his casket was closed at the funeral; there was no viewing of the body before the service began.

One of the more pleasant times I spent in the dining room occurred in 1968 when Ma brought a cute puppy home as our new family pet. The puppy was a handsome little Chihuahua that was black with tan spots over his two eyes and on his paws. That puppy soon became my best friend, supplanting Mike, the dog that I owned when I lived on Pappy's farm. Shortly after Ma brought the puppy inside the house, we all gathered around the living room table while trying to think of a name for him. We suggested names for some time. However, try as we did, none of us managed to come up with a name that everybody else liked.

Eventually, Ma wheeled herself into the kitchen for a drink of water. As she poured herself a glass of water, the perfect name suddenly came to mind. From the kitchen Ma asked, "How about Milhous?" Ma had recently read that Milhous was the middle name of Richard M. Nixon, the Republican presidential candidate in the upcoming election. As soon as she uttered the name it was warmly received by everyone present. However, none of us knew how the former vice president spelled his middle name at the time. So initially at least, we spelled the name as Milhouse. However, I never liked that spelling and subsequently changed the spelling of his name to Milhaus. In the end, Milhaus had his name and the family had a wonderful new pet.

I was as happy as a young boy could be after Milhaus came to live with us. The puppy was an immediate hit with everyone at Ma's place. However, little Milhaus was first and foremost my dog. Right from the start, he slept with me in the hallway upstairs. At least he remained with me until after I fell asleep. My brother Jeff frequently complained that he heard Milhaus running around the house at night, his little nails clicking against the hardwood floors and keeping him awake. I didn't give much credence to Jeff's complaints. As far as I was concerned, little Milhaus was a well-behaved puppy who went to bed with me every night and slept faithfully by my side until morning.

Unfortunately, Milhaus did not live a long life. Our family was used to living in the country. As such, none of us believed it was necessary to erect a fence in the backyard or to put him on a leash when letting him outside to relieve himself. That just wasn't the way things were done on Pappy's farm. One profoundly sad day in 1969, when little Milhaus was only nine months old, he was killed by a passing car while attempting to cross the highway where it passed by our house. It was Gloria who picked his lifeless body up and brought him home.

I remember crying uncontrollably as I knelt down beside my little Milhaus. Eventually, I summoned the strength to dig a grave for him in the backyard behind the garage. With tears streaming down my face, I wrapped his little body inside a white cloth that Ma had given to me for that very purpose. Then I buried my precious Milhaus. As a lasting tribute to my little friend, I placed a small headstone at the location where he was buried. I carefully maintained that headstone until the day I moved away from Ma's place to attend college at Winona State University.

Without question, the happiest moment that I ever experienced in the living room centers around the Christmas gift that I received in 1971. I was overjoyed by the absolutely perfect gift that I was given by Ma. Jennifer, Gloria, Jeff, Deloris and I had gathered with Ma in the living room that Christmas Eve. We were anxiously waiting to open our presents. In those days it was our family tradition to open all of our presents on Christmas Eve rather than on Christmas Day. As evening finally arrived, we excitedly began opening our Christmas presents.

At one point, my brother Jeff stood up, walked out of the living room and went outside the house. I had no idea what was happening, but I wasn't particularly concerned as I was busy watching everyone in the living room unwrap their presents. After a few minutes, Jeff walked back inside the house—and he was wheeling a new Rupp Roadster II mini bike inside with him! I intuitively understood the mini bike was for me and started jumping for joy! I had never dreamed of receiving such an expensive and desirable gift in my life. Not once did I dare to dream of receiving such an absolutely perfect gift. To this day that shiny new Rupp Roadster II remains the best present I ever received at Christmastime.

There aren't that many places where a kid was able to go mini biking in Wisconsin in the wintertime, so I wasn't truly able to enjoy my new present until the following spring. However, once the weather warmed enough to go riding, I was finally able to fully enjoy the mini bike that Ma had given me. There existed a small but vibrant stand of woods located on the northern side of Osseo, and several well-worn paths ran throughout the area. I still vividly remember the fun I had cruising around those paths on the Rupp Roadster II mini bike. There were only about four other kids who had mini bikes, but a lot of other kids that didn't own mini bikes joined in on the fun as well.

The individual whom I cruised around in those woods with the most was Robert Kershner. Robert had an Arctic Cat mini bike, and we often raced one another to see which one of our mini bikes was the faster of the two. Unfortunately, Robert usually won those races as his Arctic Cat really was a slightly faster mini bike than my Rupp Roadster II. Top speed wasn't always important though, as the dirt paths that we cruised around on were full of corners and curves that made it impossible for us to drive as fast as our mini bikes could go. I fondly remember how whenever two or more of us got together to ride around in those woods, we innocently imagined ourselves as a gang of badass Hells Angels, albeit, Hells Angels on mini bikes.

I spent a lot of time with Ma in the living room when I was a kid. She loved country and western music and we spent hours together there while listening to her favorite singers: Patsy Cline, Hank Williams, Loretta Lynn and Johnny Cash. More than the other artists though, we listened to Charlie Pride, who was her favorite singer. We also watched a lot of television together. Sometimes I would gently brush Ma's hair while spending time in her company. I still remember how she enjoyed it whenever I took time to brush her hair, and I was happy to share a few minutes of tenderness with her in just such a way.

We seldom missed watching a program called *ABC's Wide World of Sports* on Saturday mornings. The program was always enjoyable on those dates when a Muhammad Ali fight was scheduled, or the boxer made a personal appearance to promote one of his fights. Among our favorite moments were the humorous and sometimes intense verbal exchanges between the sportscaster Howard Cosell and Muhammad Ali. Their chemistry was electrifying, and we enjoyed watching their highly publicized and most likely choreographed confrontations a lot. Occasionally, two individuals combine to create a combined effect that is greater than the sum of their single qualities. I've always thought that the relationship between Howard Cosell and Muhammad Ali produced that kind of charismatic synergy.

Muhammad Ali was my favorite sports figure while I was growing up. Over the years though, he became much more than a sports figure to me. Muhammad Ali became a real-life hero who stood up for what he believed regardless of the consequences, and I greatly admired that quality about him. I closely followed his career both in and out of the ring in every way possible. I read virtually every book about him that was available through the inter-library loan system offered through the Osseo Public Library. I also read every article about him that I came across in sports magazines such as *Sport*, *Sports Illustrated* and *Boxing Illustrated*, etcetera. Of course, I watched all of his boxing matches when they were broadcast on *ABC's Wide World of Sports*.

My earliest recollection of Muhammad Ali goes back to the day he won the Heavyweight Championship of the World on February 25, 1964. At that time, I was about four years and nine months old. I don't actually remember the fight as I don't think anyone on Pappy's farm listened to it on the radio. However, I clearly remember the way my siblings talked incessantly about the boxing match in the days and weeks leading up to the fight. Everybody on the farm was convinced that Sonny Liston was going to destroy the less experienced Cassius Clay. Not me. I repeatedly told them that Cassius Clay was going to win and that was what happened. Some people might call that good sports intuition.

I also remember when Muhammad Ali was wrongfully stripped of his boxing title in 1967, and how three difficult years later he was finally permitted to return to the boxing ring. By that time though, he was not only a sports hero to me, he had become a larger-than-life leader and cultural phenomenon. First and foremost though, I have always thought of Muhammad Ali as the greatest boxer who ever laced up a pair of boxing gloves. His charismatic charm outside the ring was entertaining, and his political convictions were admirable, but it was his devastating athletic skills inside the boxing ring that made me think of him–as he boastfully referred to himself–as the greatest of all time! I memorized many of his poems and frequently quoted them, line for line, to my friends, classmates, family members and select members of the school faculty.

When Muhammad Ali eventually fought "Smokin' Joe" Frazier for the Heavyweight Championship of the World on March 8, 1971, their boxing match was labeled as, *"The Fight of the Century,"* and took place at Madison Square Garden in New York City. There weren't any live broadcasts of the boxing match in Osseo, but as soon as the fight ended and it was broadcast over the radio that Joe Frazier was declared the winner by a unanimous decision, I was totally outraged! To this day, I remain convinced that Muhammad Ali won the fight. Three years later, when Muhammad Ali fought George Foreman for the Heavyweight Championship of the World on October 30, 1974, the boxing match was billed as, *"The Rumble in the Jungle,"* and took place in Kinshasa, Zaire. Virtually nobody in Osseo believed Muhammad Ali had a chance against the younger and much stronger

George Foreman. Well, nobody except for me. I disagreed with my friends and all of the professional pundits who consistently predicted Muhammad Ali was going to get knocked out. I was a sophomore in high school at the time, and I placed bets with every student who was willing to put up some money. By the day of the boxing match, I had over $30.00 in bets placed with fellow students.

The fight wasn't available on live television or radio. However, there were round-by-round summaries broadcast over the radio after each round. I recall listening to those summaries with great interest as the results of each round were broadcast. When the results for the eighth round were announced and the broadcaster said Muhammad Ali had knocked George Foreman out and was once again the Heavyweight Champion of the World, I jumped for joy and shouted, "Ma! Ali won the fight!" The next day I went to school with quite the swagger in my step, and much to my pleasant surprise, all of the students that had placed a bet paid their debt in full. They also stroked my ego by acknowledging I had predicted Muhammad Ali would win the fight when nearly everyone else had said he was going to get knocked out.

Float like a butterfly, sting like a bee
The hands can't hit what the eyes can't see
Muhammad Ali

One summer Ma elected to have joint replacement surgery at a hospital in the City of Marshfield, Wisconsin. She did so after learning that new technology existed which might make it possible for her to walk again. Specifically, through receiving replacement prostheses for her damaged hips and knees. Her trusted physician, Dr. Robert Leasum did not sugarcoat the difficulties associated with the four medical procedures either. Dr. Leasum explained to her in a candid and straightforward manner that all four procedures involved having her damaged hips and knees surgically removed and replaced with artificial prostheses. He also explained to her that there would be months of often painful physical therapy to endure in the months following the four procedures. In spite of those concerns, Ma was squarely focused on the very real possibility that she might be able to walk once again.

After hearing what Dr. Leasum had to say, Ma asked for the opinions of everyone close to her, including me, before making a final decision as to whether she should have the surgical procedures. Although I was only a teenager at the time, Ma sufficiently valued my opinion as to seek my input on the subject. As if only yesterday, I remember the moment when Ma told me that there was a very real possibility that she might walk again. It was one of only a few times in my life that I witnessed Ma crying over her confinement in a wheelchair. With crippled hands she gestured at the mechanical monster beneath her. Then, with her disfigured fingers partially extended and her voice cracking from pent-up emotion she said, "I want to have the surgery, Danny, because living like this is a living hell!" Without a moment's hesitation I gave my mother a much-needed hug and replied, "Then I think you should go ahead with the surgeries, Ma!"

Ma departed for the hospital in Marshfield early in the summertime and didn't return home again for approximately two months. Gloria and Deloris visited Ma regularly throughout the time that she was away. However, I never visited her once throughout the time that she was hospitalized. Instead, I went camping. For the better part of the time that Ma was at the hospital in Marshfield, I rode my bike to Osseo every day to go to my summer job at the high school. After work I stopped by Ma's place to bathe and gather food, etcetera. Then I returned to the campsite where I ate, read and fished until it was time to go to bed.

Eventually, the day arrived when Ma returned from the hospital in Marshfield. My friend Del VanBlaricom and I had spent the better part of that day riding our bikes around while waiting for her to arrive at the house. After what seemed like an eternity, Gloria returned with her and as soon as Del and I saw Gloria's car arrive we rode our bikes to Ma's place as fast as possible. We gathered together in the living room as Ma prepared to demonstrate to everyone present the success of her multiple surgeries and the grueling weeks of intensive physical therapy that followed.

When Ma placed her walker in front of her wheelchair you could have heard a pin drop it was so silent. Nobody moved as Ma rocked back and forth in her wheelchair a couple of times to overcome the inertia holding her down. Having built up sufficient momentum, she slowly rose up from her wheelchair and put her elbows on the arm rests of the walker before her. Then, after straining to stand straight, she rested for far more than a moment as she gathered her breath and composure. Beads of sweat were forming on her brow all throughout the process. Ever so slowly, Ma moved the walker forward. She only pushed it forward a few inches. Then she slid one of her two feet forward. After another pause to gather her breath Ma, slowly slid her second foot forward. Then she repeated the process. I couldn't believe my eyes. As Ma trudged across the floor in what can only be described as a slow and laborious process, I miraculously observed my mother walking again.

Were life like a movie Ma would have successfully continued her physical therapy, regained the full strength of her legs and eventually walked on her own. She would have been able to lift her feet as she took steps rather than slide them forward. Were life that movie, Ma would have eventually tossed her walker and wheelchair aside and moved about on her own. She would have been able to go outside and enjoy walking around Osseo to visit the homes of her friends and family members. Unfortunately, life isn't a movie–and it damn sure ain't no fairytale. No, life isn't anything like that.

The rheumatoid arthritis that robbed Ma of her ability to walk about was not going to let its hold on her go that easily. The disease that had taken its toll on her defenseless joints for years was not going to let that happen. Sadly, the euphoria that filled all of our hearts that

that day soon subsided. In spite of our optimistic hopes, the multiple surgeries and the hours of painful physical therapy that she endured did not prove successful. Within a brief period of time it became increasingly difficult for Ma to put any weight down on her shoulders and arms as they rested atop the walker.

As the inflammation and pain in her shoulders and back worsened, Ma spent less and less time moving about with her walker and more and more time confined to her wheelchair. Within a span of a few months Ma quietly returned to her wheelchair where she remained for the rest of her difficult life. The emotional pain of regressing into a wheelchair for a second time had to have been extremely difficult to bear. Such an unfortunate turn of events might well have been more than most people could handle without becoming bitter. Not my mother though. Consistent with her personality, Ma patiently endured her suffering with the same grace and dignity that she displayed throughout her entire life.

When I was a teenager I occasionally took Ma for brief walks around Osseo. Occasionally getting out of the house to experience the feel of natural sunlight on her face and a gentle breeze blowing through her hair was one of Ma's simple pleasures. Most of our walks together were neighborhood outings along the streets closest to Ma's place. Ma enjoyed viewing the many well-maintained lawns in the area. She also enjoyed simple things such as watching squirrels scurry about in the oak trees and listening to songbirds chirping from the branches above. One of her favorite pleasures was listening to the cardinals and robins singing their melodic songs. She used to say they were singing exclusively for us from the safety of those treetops.

During my senior year in high school, I heard an intriguing ad on the radio station that I listened to out of Eau Claire, Wisconsin. The ad was for a live dinner performance at a place called the Fanny Hill Supper Club, a respectable restaurant and dinner theater located near the shore of the Chippewa River in Eau Claire. In truth, I no longer recall the name of the play that was advertised, but I do recall that it was a comedy and sounded like something that I thought Ma would enjoy. After giving the matter some consideration, I asked Ma on a formal date for dinner and the theater at the Fanny Hill Supper Club. Ma said yes and we made a pretty big deal out of it.

When the day of our date arrived, I donned my only sport jacket and tie, and Ma put on a pretty blue dress and her favorite necklace. We both enjoyed the dinner and the live performance and in hindsight, I strongly suspect our evening together was one of the more precious and memorable times Ma spent with any of her children. I remember feeling honored to have made that evening possible for her–to have made the evening possible for both of us. I was saddened to learn that the Fanny Hill Supper Club permanently closed in 2014.

To the rear of the living room was a short hallway that led to Ma's bedroom. Around the time of Pappy's death, Ma's physical condition rapidly deteriorated. In a brief period of no more than 10 months, she regressed from walking to walking with a cane to walking with the help of an aluminum walker to confinement in her wheelchair. The unending pain and disfigurement that Ma endured from rheumatoid arthritis, coupled with the deaths of her husband and son, took a heavy toll on her emotional well-being. Rapidly losing the ability to walk was difficult, but learning to live with increasingly limited use of her hands must have been much worse. Within a relatively brief span of time, rheumatoid arthritis had curled Ma's fingers to such an extent that they were all but shut. The disease also twisted her feet to such an extent that she could only wear slippers rather than shoes.

I still remember watching as Ma struggled to complete a number of basic functions from effectively using a pair of scissors to turning the pages of her bible to writing words down on paper. As her condition grew progressively worse, she also experienced the almost constant fatigue that is associated with rheumatoid arthritis. In response to the fatigue, Ma started taking frequent naps. As that happened I came to think of her bedroom as her sanctuary. Her bedroom became a place where she was able to find some semblance of calmness, quietude and peace of mind in spite of the nearly constant pain, suffering and fatigue that she experienced.

The last time I entered Ma's sanctuary was in 1982. I was living in Sioux Falls, South Dakota, when I received a telephone call from my older sister Margaret. She called to inform me that Ma didn't make it through kidney dialysis that morning and had passed away. After the telephone call ended, I wept for some time before regaining my composure. Then I packed my suitcase and returned to Osseo for the funeral. One of the thoughts racing through my mind as I made that long and difficult drive home again was how Ma once intimated to me that she walked in her dreams; that she wasn't confined to her wheelchair as she was while awake. I remember looking up at the white clouds that dotted the summer skies over southern Minnesota throughout the drive back and imagining her dancing.

As I traveled along the Interstate I saw her dancing gracefully among the clouds with her modest dress waving freely in the wind. Her dance partner's face was unknown and unimportant to me. I took a lot of comfort in the beautiful image of Ma dancing among those clouds. It wasn't a vision that I had or anything like that. To the contrary, I consciously willed myself to see her dancing there in that beautiful setting, and I enjoyed what I had willed myself to see for what seemed a good long while. Eventually, though, the image above disappeared into the vastness of the gradually darkening clouds I traveled beneath. I'm not sure Ma enjoyed dancing in life, but I know in my heart that she enjoyed dancing among the clouds that day. She was free of her pain and suffering and she danced like the wind.

Ma passed away from cardiogenic shock and medical complications associated with kidney failure on July 23, 1982. That was the official reason for her death. However, I intuitively knew she really died after years of suffering from rheumatoid arthritis. Ma had endured the pain and disfigurement of her affliction for far too long. She spent the last 20 or so years of her life quietly waiting for her Savior to free her from that suffering; to release her from this world into another realm of blessed tranquility and eternal rest. Helen was buried beside her husband Norman and next to her son Frederick, at the South Beef River Lutheran Cemetery on July 27, 1982.

I was grateful that Ma was given a dignified funeral service by the Reverend Robert Arneson, the same man who diligently provided pastoral care to her for years. I vividly remember how eloquently Pastor Arneson spoke about Ma at the funeral, describing her as a quiet, dignified woman who lived a good life. I found it particularly touching when the pastor said that in spite of her suffering, she hadn't been "called home" until her youngest had grown to manhood. Her purpose in this world, Pastor Arneson suggested, was to finish raising her 12 children, and Ma had at long last finished her assignment. In doing so, he suggested Ma had completed her journey through this life. On that point I wholeheartedly agreed with the good reverend's observation; Ma had successfully completed her earthly assignment.

After the funeral, there was an auction, and most of Ma's personal property and belongings were sold. Each of her children was given an opportunity to pick out a personal item that was of significance. I selected a small, alabaster elephant carving. When the auction was over and all of the visitors had left, I slowly entered Ma's sanctuary for the very last time. I intuitively understood I would never see her resting there again, or converse with her about any of life's ordinary moments. In that moment I felt truly alone for the first time in my life. After shedding several more tears in the quietude of that most beautiful space, I stepped out, closed the door, and walked away from Ma's sanctuary and the house known as place for the vert last time.

That which is loved is always beautiful
Norwegian Proverb

THE CITY OF OSSEO

One of my favorite places for us to play after moving to Osseo was an empty lot located across the street and catty-corner from the house I thought of as Ma's place. A new SuperValu grocery store would be built on that empty lot in 1972. However, for approximately the first five years that I lived in Osseo, my friends and I used that empty lot as our playground and spent countless hours there. One of the first friends I made in Osseo was my neighbor Brad Indrebo. Brad was five years older than me and as such, he was our de facto leader. In other words, Brad decided what games we played and what the rules were for those games. That said, our preferred game to play was tackle football. All of the kids in the neighborhood owned personal uniforms and helmets of varying sizes and shapes, so we were able to hit each other hard without worrying too much about getting injured.

One of the people who played football with us was quite a bit older than everyone else. His name was Bruce John Hegg, and he had what the adults said was Down Syndrome. One of Bruce's disabilities was speech-related and he pronounced his name as, "Boo DAH," with emphasis on the second syllable. As that was the way that Bruce John said his name, that was the way we pronounced it as well. Boo DAH, or Bruce John was nine years older than Brad, and at least 14 years older than me. However, despite Bruce John's actual age, he was essentially a kid at heart. Bruce John moved as slow as molasses in January, but because of his strength, he was extremely difficult for us to tackle.

Whenever the quarterback—always Brad Indrebo—handed Bruce John the football, he slowly trudged along toward the goal line as the rest of us tried desperately to take him down. We were seldom successful in those efforts. Bruce John was a touchdown-scoring machine! However, he was much more than that to us; he was our playmate and our friend. Bruce John Hegg was my friend. Statistics tell us that the average life expectancy for individuals with Down Syndrome is 60 years. Bruce John Hegg was born on May 1, 1945, and he passed away on February 17, 2005, just two months and 14 days shy of his sixtieth birthday. Subjectively speaking, that nearly 60-year life span was the only thing average about Bruce John Hegg. His purity and gentleness made him a truly exceptional human being that improved the lives of everyone who came to know him.

Approximately three blocks east of Ma's place was a residential street that everybody called Pump House Hill. The landscape in Osseo was pretty flat, and Pump House Hill was one of only a few locations in the community that had any significant incline. During the winter months, we dragged our sleds to the top of Pump House Hill and went sledding back down again at what seemed like great rates of speed at the time. Occasionally someone wiped out while sledding down the hill, and the very real danger of knowing that could happen only made things that much more exciting.

During the summer months, we did the same thing on our bikes. It was always a challenge to pedal one's bike to the top of Pump House Hill without having to get off and push. With a five-speed or even a three-speed bike, it was possible to do so, but with a one-speed bike, the attempts almost always resulted in failure. In those instances, the rider had to get off their bike and push it to the top of the street. The effort put into getting to the top of Pump House Hill was well worth it though, as the rides back down were truly exhilarating. Adding to the excitement of sledding or biking down Pump House Hill was the fact that at the bottom of the street, Pump House Hill abruptly ended where it intersected with East Street. One had to make a sharp right or left turn when reaching East Street to avoid crashing into the curb at the other side of the road and potentially wrecking one's bicycle or sled, or even getting seriously injured.

A bit farther northeast of the school building were several homes scattered about as city turned into country. In the midst of those homes, at the edge of an unsightly shale pit, stood a tiny trailer park that was owned by one of Osseo's successful businessmen named Eddie Barber. There was nothing remarkable about the place other than the fact that I eventually became friends with some of the people who lived there. Specifically, a classmate named John Back and a mysterious, unusual looking individual named Steve Matysik.

To the north of the school stood the small but vibrant stand of woods with several well-worn paths where I went mini biking when I was a kid. Those woods were supposedly off limits to us in that they were the private properties of John Ward, one of Osseo's two attorneys, and Dr. Brad Garber, one of Osseo's three medical doctors. My friends and I didn't pay particularly close attention to those property lines though, and we regularly enjoyed spending time in the woods, largely unencumbered by interference from adults.

There was also an attractive but slow-moving stream that meandered along through those woods. The body of water was officially named the North Fork Buffalo River in 1969. However, nobody that I knew of ever referred to the stream by that name. Instead, they called it the Buffalo River. The official name notwithstanding, the Buffalo River is more of a gentle stream than a river. One summer day my friend Donald Keffer took me swimming in an easily accessible area of that stream. Up to that time, I had never been in a body of water larger than a bathtub and couldn't swim a single stroke. So, although the water was no more than 18 inches deep, the current slow, and the riverbed soft and sandy, I was truly frightened as we stepped from the shore into the water.

My fears may have been justified, for shortly after stepping into the water I lost my footing on the soft riverbed and fell backward into the water. Suddenly, I panicked as the water that covered me filled my nose and mouth. I tried to lift my head above the water but as I attempted to do so my feet slipped again and down I went for the second time. By then I was choking from sucking in water where I thought there would be air. As if only yesterday, I remember the way

Donald laughed throughout the entire event. Fortunately, I managed to eventually regain my footing, stand upright and catch my breath. Donald undoubtedly saw the entire incident as harmless. However, it wasn't such a laughing matter to me. I thought I was going to drown right then and there.

After crawling out of the water I vowed to never go swimming again until I learned how to swim. Later that same day, I asked Ma to enroll me in swimming lessons and she agreed to do so. I ended up taking swimming lessons for two years. Learning how to swim was difficult for me at first in that I was deathly afraid of the water. However, as time passed and my fear of the water subsided, I became a pretty good swimmer and grew to love being in and around the water. Although I eventually learned to enjoy swimming in creeks and streams, I always preferred the controlled environment that swimming pools provided a lot more.

Suddenly, an almost overwhelming desire to enjoy a cup of coffee brought me back to the present, and I decided it was time to take short drive out to one of the restaurants located near the Interstate 94 exit to purchase a cup or two. The first restaurant I saw was a McDonald's so that was where I stopped. As I approached I was surprised to see how different everything looked. For one thing, there was a stoplight along US Highway 10. When I grew up in Osseo, there weren't any stop-lights to be found. Likewise, most of the businesses that I saw were unfamiliar to me. After purchasing a cup of piping hot coffee at McDonald's, I sat down and began thinking back at the way the area looked in my youth.

When I moved to the City of Osseo in 1967, there were two highways running through the community. One was US Highway 10, which passed directly by Ma's place. The other was US Highway 53. A new highway was about to open on the eastern outskirts of Osseo called Interstate 94, and various sections of the Interstate highway had been under construction since 1965. However, the Osseo exit didn't officially open until November 1967. The opening of the Interstate radically changed the character of Osseo, and I witnessed most of it first-hand while growing up. First and foremost among those changes were the multitude of new businesses that opened near the Interstate. Those businesses created a positive economic impact that helped the community in countless ways. However, the unintended consequence of the Interstate's arrival was that it also brought about the closing of several other businesses located in downtown Osseo.

The first of the new businesses to open out near the Interstate was a Sunoco Service Station–which later became a DX. A Texaco Service Station opened in June of 1970, and later that same year, the new Standard Service Station opened for business. Three restaurants opened near the Interstate as well. The first restaurant was called the Big Steer and it opened in 1971. The second restaurant was called the Bail-I-Wick and construction on it began in October 1972. The third restaurant, called the Alan House, was physically attached to the Best Western motel that opened in 1974. For the most part, both the Alan House and Big Steer served fast food and catered to families that were traveling along the Interstate. I worked part-time as a dishwasher at the Big Steer while going to high school and as a short-order cook at the Alan House while attending college.

Unlike the Big Steer and Alan House restaurants, the Bail-I-Wick was a decidedly upscale establishment that catered to local professionals. Unfortunately, the Bail-Wick restaurant went out of business in 1979. However, the establishment reopened some time later as The Osseo Inn. The new owners added a small bowling alley in an effort to draw additional business. The Osseo Inn continued as a steakhouse, lounge and bowling ally for nearly two decades before it closed for good in the late 1990s. The building was subsequently demolished in 1998. The Alan House and Big Steer restaurants also went out of business in the 1990s.

At the northwestern edge of Osseo, off County Road NN, was North

Street. That road led to an unattractive part of Osseo referred to as the industrial park. The buildings in that area were made from brick and most of them appeared old and dilapidated. However, at one time they were all thriving businesses that provided employment for many of the residents living in and around Osseo. One of the businesses that existed on Elevator Street was the Osseo Elevator Company, one of two feed mills that served area farmers. One of the larger buildings on the street was once home to a business called the Osseo Canning Company, but often referred to as the pea factory.

The pea factory canned a variety of vegetables that were grown in the area. The building was constructed at its specific location because an artesian well existed there. A lot of clean water is used in the canning process, and it made good business sense to construct the plant at a location with a seemingly unlimited supply of fresh water available. The Osseo Canning Company went out of business before I moved to Osseo in 1967. However, another business called the Electric Cleaner Company opened inside a part of the larger building in the early 1960s and is still in operation as of 2023.

Another business on Elevator Street was the Osseo Silo Company, which opened in 1962. It produced concrete staves that were used in the construction of concrete silos on dairy farms throughout the area. The handsome silos were distinctively marked with a red and white checkerboard pattern that circled around the top. The Osseo Silo Company went out of business in 1993. Another business that once existed in the industrial park was the United Milk Products Company. However, it was located on Condensery Road rather than Elevator Street. Virtually everyone in Osseo referred to the United Milk Products Company as the Condensery. Regardless of its name, the Condensery produced condensed and evaporated milk, the primary difference being that evaporated milk is unsweetened and condensed milk is heavily sweetened. The Condensery was built in 1920, and it was Osseo's largest employer for nearly half a century before it became financially insolvent and closed in 1965.

At one time there was a small train station in Osseo that was situated in the area where Condensery Road and Elevator Street converge. Railway service arrived in Osseo as far back as 1887 and continued until the line was abandoned in 1975. I can remember the trains as if it was yesterday. My friend Steve Erickson and I sometimes played along those railroad tracks when we were kids. Once we heard the sound of a train in the distance we placed pennies on the tracks and waited for the train to pass over them. Afterwards, we picked up what had previously been copper pennies and marveled at the way they had flattened into wafer thin discs that were slightly curved into the oval shape of the track's steel rails.

A short distance beyond the industrial park, immediately to the west of Condensery Road and to the north of US Highway 10 stood Hong Lumber Company. To the east of Condensery Road on the north side of US Highway 10 was the North Star Service Station, one of the five gas stations that served Osseo when I moved there in 1967. In that same area was the Osseo Car Wash and Osseo Laundromat. The next business on the north side of the highways was the Standard Service Station. It was at that intersection where the two highways diverged, with US Highway 10 continuing east and US Highway 53 turning to the south.

On the other side of the street from the Standard Service Station stood the Osseo Evangelical Lutheran Church, a simple wooden structure that was built in the 1890s. Until the time of our move to Osseo, I'd always assumed that Pappy had been baptized, confirmed and buried at the South Beef River Lutheran Church. However, after the move, I learned that he became a member of the Osseo Evangelical Lutheran Church after his family moved to a dairy farm located near Osseo in Eau Claire County. So in much the same way that Pappy did, I began attending worship services at the Osseo Evangelical Lutheran Church after our family moved to Osseo. Located directly behind the wooden church was a brick building that was constructed in the late 1950s. Inside that building was where I attended both my Sunday school and confirmation classes. A new Lutheran church was constructed on the south side of Osseo in 1972, and when the new church opened I began attending worship services and confirmation classes at that location.

In the same area as the Hong Lumber company, but on the south side of US Highway 10, was a business called the Osseo Co-op Creamery. The creamery opened in 1920 and processed milk that it purchased from area dairy farmers. The creamery went out of business in 1981. At that time the building was sold and converted into Curt's Auto Body. The next business in that area was the Conoco Service Station. My friend Christopher Hagen briefly owned and operated that business, having purchased it shortly after graduating from the Osseo-Fairchild High School in 1971. However, Christopher had to sell the business when he was drafted into the Army in 1972.

Another building in that area was an apartment building known as the Flats. Nearly everybody understood the Flats were occupied by some of Osseo's least fortunate residents. A classmate of mine named John Back and his mother, Myra, were two of the residents living there when I moved to Osseo in 1967. Myra married a gentleman named Aloizy Kiehl a short time later and their plans were set to move into a house and begin their new life together. However, as tragedy would have it, Mr. Kiehl sustained a severe brain injury within days of their marriage. As the medical bills mounted and their family income evaporated, Aloizy, Myra and John ended up moving from the modest apartment they lived in at the Flats to a tiny trailer located in Eddie Barber's Trailer Court.

The next business on the south side of US Highway 10 going east was a small grocery store called Waldo's. As a kid, I had little interest in the grocery store itself. However, the proprietor of the business was a kindly gentleman named Waldo Johnson, and he was active in several community activities including Little League baseball. Although I seldom played, I fondly remember one particular game. On the day of the game Mr. Johnson noticed his starting shortstop wasn't present when the game was about to start. At the very last minute, Mr. Johnson looked at me and said, "Severson, you're playing shortstop today." Little did he realize it when he put me in the game, but I'm left-handed.

As everyone who has played baseball knows, shortstops are usually right-handed. That is because they are positioned between the third baseman and the second-base bag, and must be able to pick up infield grounders and throw them to the first baseman as quickly as possible. A left-handed player at the position of shortstop has to adjust their body in a certain way before throwing the ball to the first baseman, and that slight delay can slow down the play at first base. Fortunately for me, and much to Mr. Johnson's credit, he didn't take me out of the ball game after realizing I was left-handed. But what really made that event a memorable for me is that from that day forward, Waldo Johnson referred to me as Lefty. Years later, whenever I returned to Osseo and ran into him somewhere, he said, "Hi Lefty, what has my favorite left-handed shortstop been up to lately?" Sadly, Mr. Johnson passed away on September 16, 2014.

The next business, located at the divergence of US Highway 10 and US Highway 53, was the Mobil Service Station, and across the street from there was the Osseo Motel. Then, about one block further east was Central Park. Although smaller than a city block, I nevertheless thought of Central Park as an attractive park with several mature oak trees situated throughout. Of course, as was always the case in Osseo, there were also a few unattractive pine trees scattered throughout the park. Interspersed between the trees were several picnic tables, and I spent many a summer afternoon resting on them while reading books or listening to music on my cassette tape player.

One block east of Central Park stood the United Church of Christ, which was the only other church in Osseo in 1967. The handsome brick church was constructed in the 1920s. Although it was fair to say that the United Church of Christ was the more attractive of the two churches in Osseo, almost everyone in the community belonged to the larger Lutheran congregation. In fact, I only knew a few people who worshiped at the United Church of Christ. Directly to the south of Central Park was the City Hall Building, a structure that was built of an unattractive yellowish-colored brick in 1938. Of course, at that time the building was called the Osseo Village Hall. It wasn't until 1941 that the name was officially changed to the City Hall Building.

There were large doors on the east side of the building where the fire trucks for the all-volunteer Fire Department were parked. Inside the building's basement were various city offices such as the mayor and clerk. The basement also housed the library, which consisted of two tiny rooms. Although the library was small by any measure, I was able to check out a variety of books that one might not ordinarily expect to find in a small, conservative community such as Osseo. For example, I was able to read a number of controversial yet interesting books with titles such as: *The Communist Manifesto* by Karl Marx and Friedrich Engels, *Soul on Ice* by Eldridge Cleaver, *Quotations from Chairman Mao Tse-Tung,* and *The Autobiography of Malcolm X.* Not everything I read was of a controversial nature though. I also read a lot of books about camping and the outdoors, and I'm certain that I read every book that had been written up to that point about my hero, Muhammad Ali.

By far the most interesting feature of the City Hall Building was the gymnasium located on the main floor. Although quite old, the gym was always kept clean and orderly by a reclusive maintenance man named Eddie Kolden, a kindly individual who had a purple birthmark that covered well over half his face. Mr. Kolden was as friendly as the day is long and always willing to help others. For a certain time while I was growing up, the gymnasium was open Saturday mornings for recreation. Kids of all ages showed up to play basketball and a variety of other games. In hindsight, I'm sure there were concerned adults from the community who organized these activities as well as supervised them, but they kept a very low profile, and as far as I could tell, it seemed as though the kids were the only people there during Saturday morning recreation.

Another activity that I enjoyed even more than Saturday morning recreation was attending the dances held inside the gymnasium on Saturday nights. The dances weren't free, but they were always affordable and entertaining. For a time, various bands performed at the City Hall Building. However, that changed over time as a local band named Sage emerged as everybody's favorite. They were so superior to all of the other bands that performed in those days that they became the only band the people wanted to hear. Sage consisted of three brothers: Randy, Gary and Mark Anderson. A supremely talented vocalist named Shari Otto sang with them from time to time as well. Other individuals may have been in the band at certain times, but I do not remember their names.

The band Sage became so popular around Osseo that the term "Sage Dance" developed into a part of the local vocabulary, supplanting the more generic term of dance. For example, people no longer told their friends there was going to be a dance at the City Hall Building next weekend. Instead, they said there was going to be a Sage Dance at the City Hall building next weekend. Whenever there was a Sage Dance in Osseo, people from miles away showed up to listen to their music and dance the night away. Sage only played rock and roll songs in the years that I lived in Osseo. However, years later the band introduced a lot of country and western music into their act.

Although Sage had legions of devoted fans located throughout west central Wisconsin, there was never any doubt as to who their number one fan was. That venerable distinction went to an individual named Tommy "Tom Cat" Olson. Tommy lived with his extremely patient parents, Kenneth and Constance, on their dairy farm located adjacent to the South Beef River Lutheran Church. The name on his official birth certificate read Thomas. However, virtually everybody in the City of Osseo knew him as Tommy, or Tom Cat. Although Tommy exhibited what was commonly referred to as severe mental retardation in the 1970s, his always gregarious and often outrageous personality endeared him to everyone in Osseo. Over time he became something of a local legend.

Tom Cat attended every Sage Dance held at the City Hall Building. Whenever the band performed their cover of the instrumental, "Wipe Out," by The Ventures, Tommy went into full-throttle dance mode. The crowd on the dance floor formed a circle around him as he started dancing wildly to the music. Then the crowd enthusiastically cheered Tom Cat on by encouraging him to dance faster and faster until such time as he was literally spinning around on the dance floor. I have often thought that Tom Cat Olson, the legend of Osseo, Wisconsin, was America's first breakdancer!

Tommy also saw himself as an important law enforcement officer. He somehow obtained a faux detective badge from a mail-order catalogue that he kept with him, secured safely inside his wallet. He often flashed the badge at people and introduced himself to them as, "Detective Steve McGarrett, Hawaii Five-O." It wasn't the least bit unusual to see Tommy directing students to wait at a crosswalk until he gave the signal for them to cross the street with caution. Most of Osseo's residents had a good-natured laugh while watching Tom Cat perform in his role as Detective Steve McGarrett. However, not all of the community's residents thought it was funny. The Chief of Police was a gentleman named Steve Peterson, and he interpreted Tommy's actions as an unlawful attempt at impersonating a police officer. The Chief of Police was technically correct of course, but everyone else in the community saw no harm in Tommy Olson's entertaining antics.

Tommy's mother Constance passed away on March 1, 1986, and he understandably took the loss very hard. Fortunately for Tommy, his father Kenneth "Kenny" Olson was there for him to provide the same kind of love and unending patience that his mother exhibited. Sadly, his father Kenneth passed away at 91 years of age on October 1, 2018.

When Tommy's father Kenny passed away, his sister Christie became his guardian and he started living with her. Unfortunately, Tommy grew frustrated over the loss of his father's companionship as well as no longer living on his father's dairy farm, the only place he had ever lived. Eventually, the situation became untenable and Christie had to make the difficult decision to relinquish her guardianship. Since that time, Tommy has lived in a number of group homes. He is reportedly doing well as of 2022. Various members of the congregation at South Beef River Lutheran Church remain in contact with him and send him care packages. They also send him gifts at Christmastime.

To the northwest of the City Hall Building was the City of Osseo's water tower, a behemoth concrete structure that was built in 1928. Unlike modern water towers that are hour-glass shaped, with a larger water reservoir at the top, a slender middle with a wider base again at the bottom, Osseo's water tower was the exact same thickness from top to bottom. When I moved to Osseo in 1967, I saw that enormous structure as a concrete monolith that reached high into the heavens. It was unquestionably Osseo's most distinctive landmark. Much to my chagrin or annoyance, that handsome monolith was torn down some years later as so much concrete and rebar and replaced with one of those generic, hour-glass shaped water towers. The nondescript new water tower was constructed in 1983.

There was a mysterious white building located immediately behind the Osseo Motel called the Masonic Lodge. I did not and still don't know what went on inside the building. After the Masonic Lodge was an automobile parts store called Fairchild Auto Supply. Years later that auto parts store moved to Seventh Street, but is was located on US Highway 53 when I moved to Osseo. South of Fairchild Auto Supply was a beauty shop and next to that was one of Osseo's five bars, an establishment called the Oasis.

Next to the Oasis was a grocery store officially known as the Red & White. However, Ma referred to the business as Nig's. A gentleman named Eddie Anderson worked at Nig's, and his daughter Lori and I were classmates. On the other side of US Highway 53, south of the Mobil Service Station, was the A&W Drive-In, an old-fashioned root beer stand with no indoor seating. There were a few stools positioned at the counter where kids could sit and enjoy a cold root beer along with their hamburger and some fries, and that was where I always sat when I ate there. However, just about everybody who dined at the A&W Drive-In did so while sitting in their car.

Past the drive-in, still going south on US Highway 53, was Osseo's only automobile dealership, a business called Gunderson Chevrolet. The next business was a store called the SuperValu, one of Osseo's three groceries. The owner of the SuperValu was a gentleman named Roger Swett. He later constructed a new SuperValu located across the street and catty-corner from Ma's place in 1972. Directly behind the SuperValu was a small women's clothing store called Bye's Dress Shop. Later, when the SuperValu moved to its location near Ma's place, Bye's Dress Shop expanded into the old building. A wellness business opened at that location in 2022. Behind Bye's going west on Seventh Street stood Midwest Farm Supply. I worked there when I was in high school. We installed silo unloaders on top of empty silos. I vividly recall how frightening it was climbing to the top of an empty silo to assemble the metal tripods that the unloaders were attached to.

Across Seventh Street from the SuperValu, back on the west side of US Highway 53, was the Beef River Farmer's Union, a cooperative feed mill that stood on the northern bank of the South Fork Buffalo River. That feed mill was the business where Pappy hauled his corn and oats to have it ground into feed. Incidentally, the reason the Beef River Farmer's Union and South Beef River Lutheran Church have different names than the river beside them is that prior to 1930, the Buffalo River was called the Beef River.

Smack dab in the center of Osseo was Lake Martha, an admittedly small but attractive lake. The lake was named after Martha Field, the wife of one of Osseo's earliest and most influential entrepreneurs, a gentleman named Stoddard Field. The lake was created by damming the South Fork Buffalo River where it crosses beneath US Highway 53, in the area of the Beef River Farmer's Union cooperative. Lake Martha was an admittedly attractive body of water. However, very few of Osseo's residents went swimming in the lake due to the fact that the water was always murky and muddy just beneath the surface.

Several kids played ice hockey on Lake Martha throughout the winter months. I never participated in those games. However, I frequently hung out at the lake while those hockey matches were played. My friend Paul Keffer was arguably the best hockey player in Osseo. He seemed to fly across the ice as quickly as the north wind blows on his pair of skates. Interestingly enough, Paul played hockey with figure skates as his parents told him they couldn't afford to purchase a pair of more costly hockey skates. My friend Jeff Olson and his older brother Chris were two other exceptionally talented hockey players.

As with swimming, very few people went fishing on Lake Martha, and that was largely due to the condition of the water, which was by all accounts unhealthy. Over time the condition of the water in Lake Martha became so poor that a renovation project was undertaken to save the lake. The restoration project involved first draining the lake and then dredging the bottom. At the same time the lake was drained, several repairs were made to the dam. With all of the improvements completed, the City of Osseo decided to initiate a new annual celebration called Lake Martha Days. The first Lake Martha Days celebration was held in Osseo in July 1981.

From above the dam, Lake Martha was calm and relaxing. However, below the bridge, where rushing water flowed over the dam, things were always loud and misty. Although prohibited from doing so, the Keffer kids and I sometimes walked behind the water that spilled over the dam to catch crayfish. I don't believe we ever did anything with the crayfish we caught except keep them in buckets and play with them. Perhaps it was the perceived danger of getting pinched by one of their claws that made catching them so much fun. I don't know. All I remember is that we had a lot of fun engaging in that activity.

There was also reasonably good fishing in the area below the dam, especially in an area located directly before the confluence of the North Fork and South Fork of the Buffalo River. As a kid, I spent a fair amount of my time fishing for trout in that area. However, I spent a lot more time walking along the well-worn paths found throughout the wooded area. One of my pleasant memories of walking about there involves an unexpected encounter with a mud puppy. While casually walking past a stand of tall marsh grass, a large salamander crossed the path directly in front of me. I later learned the animal was a mud puppy. I didn't realize such an animal existed up to that point, and I remember being quite startled when I first observed it passing by. However, curiosity quickly got the best of me and I ended up watching it until it slithered back into the marsh and out of my view.

On the opposite side of the Buffalo River from the Farmer's Union was an abandoned garage, and next to that was Royce Olson's Dairy. Similar businesses probably don't exist any longer. However, Royce Olson made his living delivering dairy products to people living in and around Osseo. In that same area was a tiny warehouse operated by the city's beer distributor. The two most popular beers in Osseo in those days were Walter's beer, brewed in Eau Claire, Wisconsin, and Leinenkugel's beer, brewed in Chippewa Falls, Wisconsin.

A bit farther to the south of that warehouse, but still on the western side of US Highway 53, was the Gulf Service Station. In that same area, but on the eastern side of US Highway 53, stood Dan's Drive-In. Not long after I moved to Osseo, a woman named Lueann Yule purchased the restaurant and changed the name to Lueann's Drive-In. With Ma no longer able to make meals at home, I enjoyed countless orders of hamburgers, cheeseburgers and pizza burgers with french fries at Pepsi Cola at Lueann's Drive-In throughout my youth and teenage years. Lueann retired in 1978, and at that time she sold the restaurant. Still later, the restaurant went out of business.

On the other side of Osseo from Lueann's Drive-In were the eastern and southeastern parts of the community. My recollection is that there was only one business in the area and it was called Colby's Florist Shop. I purchased flowers for Ma there when young, but otherwise, I had no interest in going there. The southeastern part of Osseo is also the area where the Osseo Area Municipal Hospital, a tiny one-story medical facility was located. Adjacent to the hospital was the Osseo Area Nursing Home. They both opened in 1964. My sister Dorothy gave birth to the first baby delivered at that hospital, a girl named Pam Maug. Osseo was a small enough community that the Tri-County News wrote an entire article about the event.

I was never inside the hospital. However, I spent time at the nursing home visiting with people who were important to me. My maternal grandparents, Martin H. and Olena G. Hanson, both lived at the Osseo Area Nursing Home. Ma gently instructed me to visit with them from time to time, and whenever she did I stopped by for a few minutes. Also, my paternal grandparents, Sigurd and Bertha Severson, lived in a house that was located only a short distance from the nursing home. Whenever Ma reminded me to visit one set of grandparents, I usually stopped for a brief visit with the other set of grandparents as well. In hindsight, I wish I would have visited with all four of them several more times....

I only have a few memories of visiting grandpa and grandma Hanson at the Osseo Area Nursing Home. Unfortunately, grandpa Hanson had dementia and didn't realize I was visiting with him. Fortunately, grandma Hanson was always alert whenever I visited with her. She was a gentle and sweet woman who truly appreciated my stopping by for a visit. As with Ma, she was confined to a wheelchair. One thing that I found unusual about her, at least from a child's perspective, was the fact that one of her feet dangled freely from her leg. Grandma had broken the bone in her leg so many times that it would no longer heal. So, grandma Hanson's foot dangled freely from her leg, held in place by flesh, muscle and cartilage, but not bone. Another fond memory that I have of her is the way she pursed her lips when she smiled.

I also enjoyed visiting grandpa and grandma Severson at their home in Osseo. Grandpa Severson appeared very old and tired. He sat in his recliner by the living room window. I remember that he didn't speak to me very much. Grandpa Severson was content to stare out his living room window. Perhaps he was reflecting on his youth when he did so. All I know is that grandpa didn't have much to say. Grandma Severson, on the other hand, was an exceptionally spry woman who always engaged in friendly conversation during our visits. I still remember how she provided tasty snacks every time I visited with her, usually generous plates of cookies or cake served with a big glass of ice-cold milk. I also remember her speaking with an extremely thick, almost musical Norwegian accent.

In addition to the tiny Central Park mentioned previously, there was another larger park located on the south side of Osseo. Not too far past Dan's Drive-In was Stoddard Park. Early in Osseo's history, an entrepreneur named Stoddard Field owned most of the land in that area. Then, as early as 1916, and continuing through 1920, Mr. Field divided much of his land into parcels and sold it to others for profit. After selling most of the land, Stoddard Field donated a large section of his remaining land to the community. That undeveloped stretch of land eventually became Stoddard Park.

There were two ways of entering Stoddard Park. When driving a car, a visitor had to turn east off of US Highway 53, onto Park Avenue and continue in an easterly direction for three blocks until reaching the park. The other entrance was near to the eastern edge of Osseo, just off County Road B. To enter the park via the eastern entrance, a visitor had to walk or ride their bicycle over what was then a gravel pathway that connected two well-maintained footbridges. Those two footbridges led the visitor over an attractive but marshy part of the Buffalo River where it fed into Lake Martha.

My favorite memory of entering Stoddard Park via those footbridges has to do with the plethora of frogs, pollywogs and dragonflies that I found in abundance throughout the area. Most of the frogs were less than an inch long. However, others were enormous bullfrogs. My friends and I spent a lot of carefree time chasing and catching the pollywogs and frogs. We'd always let them go again before going on our way, but the challenge of catching them was always entertaining. When we weren't busy chasing frogs and pollywogs, we sometimes watched fish feeding upon the mosquitos and other insects that flew about above the water. It wasn't uncommon to see them jump out of the water to snatch an insect from the air.

Stoddard Park was my favorite place to go in Osseo. At the southern edge of Stoddard Park, when entering from US Highway 53, stood a building known as the Cabin in the Pines. Scouting events, wedding receptions and family reunions were held there throughout the year. The Cabin in the Pines was also home to the American Legion Carl Nelson Post 324, the American Legion Auxiliary Post 324, and the Veterans of Foreign Wars Post 8514.

The Cabin was constructed in 1933, but has consistently been well-maintained over the years and looks much newer than it is. Resting as it does among a stand of mature pine trees, the Cabin in the Pines is a handsome sight to see. That end of the park featured a small wooded area that was enclosed by a circular road. Families frequently enjoyed holding picnics and other social events in that area. There was always plenty of room for play and other activities on the well-maintained grassy area found there amongst the mature trees.

By the eastern end of the park, not far from the previously mentioned footbridges, stands a softball field that was maintained by the Carl Nelson Post 324 of the American Legion. The post is named for Carl

Nelson, an Osseo man who was killed in action during World War I. The Carl Nelson Post was involved in many activities in and around Stoddard Park when I was growing up, but the softball park may very well have been their most visible contribution. Softball was a wildly popular sport in those days and there were fast-pitch and slow-pitch leagues for both men and women. As previously mentioned, I played Little League baseball on that field in my youth. What I admired the most about that softball field though, was the way that it paid homage to the City of Osseo's lone casualty of the Vietnam conflict, a young man named Craig S. Olson.

The softball park had fallen into some disrepair by the time I moved to Osseo in 1967. Therefore, the entire surface of the playing field was redone in 1975, with new fencing and floodlights installed at the same time. A new concession stand and modern bathroom facilities were also installed. What I liked best about the many improvements, though, was that there beside the attractive new softball field and concession stand stood a flagpole with a plaque installed at the base that honored the fallen young soldier. Specialist 4th Class Craig S. Olson was killed in action at Tay Ninh Provence, South Vietnam, on January 7, 1969. His service was further honored when the Veterans of Foreign Wars Post 8514 formally obtained permission from the family of Craig S. Olson to rename the VFW post after him in 1986.

Located only a short distance away from the softball field was a large metal building called the Palladium Ballroom. As with the softball park, the Palladium was maintained by the Carl Nelson Post of the American Legion. When the Palladium was first constructed it was little more than a pole shed with a concrete floor. However, over the years the Palladium Ballroom was upgraded with a wooden dance floor, a modern bar and a number of interior improvements that made it an attractive-looking establishment–at least on the inside. Sadly, the Palladium Ballroom collapsed after a severe snowstorm hit Osseo early on the morning of Sunday, February 24, 2019. The damage was so extensive that the building could not be repaired.

Although Stoddard Park had many interesting places and features, the most exciting place to be, at least from my perspective as a kid, was the Municipal Swimming Pool. The pool that was in existence when I moved to Osseo in 1967 was little more than a rectangular stretch of concrete with a shallow end, a deep end, and a rope running across the middle that separated the two halves. I sometimes referred to it as the cement pond when I was a kid, which is what the swimming pool on the television program *The Beverly Hillbillies* was called. It was at the "cement pond" where I first took swimming lessons after nearly drowning in the North Fork Buffalo River.

The old pool was torn down in 1971 and subsequently replaced by a newer and larger pool on year later. The new pool was considered state-of-the-art in that it was equipped with modern features such as two diving boards, bathrooms, shower areas, and two large clothes changing areas. The pool even had drinking fountains. I remember how happy the Keffer kids and I were when the new pool opened in May 1972. I think we went swimming there every day for a month once it opened.

In addition to the restaurants located in the City of Osseo, there were two other dining establishments located a short distance outside of the city limits when I moved to Osseo in 1967. To the east of Osseo, on US Highway 10, stood Vi's Supper Club, a business owned by a woman named Viola Steen. Viola subsequently sold the business to a gentleman named Robert "Bobby" Klick in 1971, and at that time the name was changed to Klick's Supper Club. I was classmates with his daughter Cindy. Mr. Klick later sold the business when he retired in 1977, and since that time the supper club has changed ownership several times.

To the west of Osseo on US Highway 53 was another restaurant and bar called the Chief Inn. The establishment was owned and operated by Arthur "Red" Peterson and his wife Marion from 1950 until their retirement in 1973. A good friend of mine named Steve Erickson and his parents frequently dined at the Chief Inn on weekends. One time his parents invited me along. The deep-fried haddock was delicious. Ownership of the popular establishment changed several times before it finally burned down in August 1997.

After enjoying a couple cups of piping hot coffee, I decided to visit the downtown area and stop at the Norske Nook restaurant for a slice of delicious rhubarb pie. Fortunately, the taste of the pie was every bit as delicious as I had hoped it would be. As I enjoyed the pie, I couldn't help but take notice how the downtown area wasn't at all how I remembered it from my youth. Several of the buildings were gone and others had new facades which made them unrecognizable.

DOWNTOWN

As previously described, there were several businesses located at different locations throughout the City of Osseo when I moved there in 1967. However, the vast majority of them were concentrated along both sides of Seventh Street. Going east on the north side of Seventh Street, from where it intersected with US Highway 53, stood a tiny men's clothing store called Gilbert's Clothing. That was the store where Ma purchased the suit that I wore at Pappy's funeral. It was also the store where Ma purchased my school clothes when I was in grade school.

The next store going east was Si Johnson's Hardware. At one point when I was wrapped up in the sport of boxing, I became obsessed with the idea of building a regulation-size boxing ring and organizing some fights. I bamboozled Ma into purchasing enough rope for the ring from Si Johnson's Hardware. Later, when Ma figured out what I had done, she became visibly angry with me over the way I tricked her into making the purchase. I would like to say that her response to what I did made me feel bad. However, that wasn't the case. I was pleased as punch to have succeeded in getting all of the materials I needed to construct a regulation-size boxing ring, and I felt anything but remorseful over what I had done.

The boxing ring that I built received a lot of use over the next few years at locations both in and around Osseo. Initially, I set it up in the backyard at Ma's place. However, the most popular location for holding boxing matches was in the middle of a vegetable garden at the home of my friend Robert Kershner. His father was a gentleman named Russell, and for a time at least, he allowed Robert and me to set up the boxing ring in the middle of his garden–but only after he finished harvesting his vegetables. Due to the location of the ring, I billed the boxing matches held there as taking place at Kershner's Square Garden, a not-so-subtle nod to the more famous venue in New York City known as Madison Square Garden.

Robert and I loved boxing, and we took part in several knock-down drag-out matches against one another over the years. As previously stated, we also raced mini bikes quite a few times. And while Robert won most of the mini bike races, I won the majority of our boxing matches. Robert was a traditional right-handed boxer who moved to the left and right with a classic shuffle. My boxing style was much less conventional. For one thing I was a southpaw, and that alone made my style unusual. I remained flat-footed when I boxed, but I wasn't a classic slugger inasmuch as I didn't possess the upper body strength necessary for that style. Nor did I bob and weave from side to side as boxers who shuffle around the ring usually do. Instead, I tended to stand upright while bending my torso backward and forward and using my arms to block my opponent's hooks, jabs and uppercuts.

From my admittedly subjective perspective, our most competitive fight was our last boxing match. The seven-round bout took place at Kershner's Square Garden one warm November weekend less than a month after Muhammad Ali regained the heavyweight championship of the world by knocking George Foreman out in Kinshasa, Zaire. On the humorous side of things, shortly before Robert and I were ready to begin our fight we went inside his parents house and changed into our boxing trunks. For some reason Robert could not locate his boxing trunks anywhere, so he hastily grabbed a pair of boxer shorts from his father's dresser drawer to wear during the fight. Fortunately for him, nobody present seemed to notice he was wearing his dad's underwear. My boxing trunks were the same solid white color as well, and that may have been one of the reasons why nobody took notice.

Something I always tried to do whenever I started a boxing match was to rush out to the center of the ring and punch my opponent right in the face. By doing so, I was letting my opponent know that I meant business and was not afraid of them. As though the boxing match happened only yesterday, I remember hearing the bell sound and rushing out to meet Robert in just such a way. However, Robert must have known what I was going to do as he quickly sidestepped my punch and threw a powerful right hook of his own that caught me on the jaw. Robert's punch struck with greater force than any punch I had received since getting the hell beat out of me in a previous boxing match by a classmate named Brian Matye. After getting punched in the face by Robert I reminded myself of that loss and told myself that I needed to summon every bit of strength, courage and determination I had in me if I wanting to avoid another embarrassing loss similar to the one handed to me by Brian Matye.

For the next seven rounds Robert and I figuratively went toe-to-toe. Robert quickly settled into the classic boxing style referenced above. However, it took me a couple of rounds to find my rhythm. Unlike in our previous fights, Robert was holding his gloves close to his chest with his elbows pointing out to the left and right. I was somewhat confused by the way that he held his gloves and failed to land many punches. Nevertheless, as he shuffled to the right and left I pursued him relentlessly. Every so often Robert was able to sting my face with lightening quick jabs and an occasional uppercut. However, I managed to successfully avoid most of his punches by bending my torso back at the waist or blocking them by using my gloved hands and forearms. Although it was obvious that Robert had grown a lot stronger than me since our previous fight, I was still substantially faster, and I used that to my advantage.

Every so often throughout the fight, Robert shuffled to one side or the other and left himself open in the process. Whenever that happened I utilized my superior speed to land a solid left hook or right jab. My jabs weren't powerful enough to hurt Robert. However, every time they landed I scored points. As I recall, Wendell Pederson was the referee for the fight. However, I can't remember who the two judges were. What I vividly remember is that when the boxing match finally ended, I was declared the winner by a split decision. I'm sure the people watching the fight who wanted Robert to win thought he should have won the match–and they may have been right. However, those judging the fight awarded the victory to me.

Regardless of the final decision, I knew right then and there that the fight against Robert Kershner was going to be my last boxing match. When I started boxing as a kid, the punches didn't hurt very much. However, after my friends and I passed through puberty we grew significantly stronger and the punches started hurting. In fact, they hurt a lot! When Robert's dad told us to take the ring down a few days later, I packed everything up and brought it back to Ma's place. I no longer remember what happened to the regulation-size boxing ring that I talked Ma into purchasing for me. However, I kept my leather boxing gloves. In fact, they were still proudly on display at my home in Oklahoma until 2010, when I entered retirement.

Next to the hardware store was the Bank of Osseo and then Vold's Barber Shop. Next came the Farmer's Store, an old-fashioned general store that sold a variety of products for adults that were of little or no interest to me. However, they sold candy (Kraft caramel squares were my candy of choice), Pepsi Cola and Coca-Cola, albums, 45's and cigarettes. The Farmer's Store was located in the Hagen and Waller Building, one of the oldest structures on Seventh Street. The brick building was constructed by Ed Hagen and Oliver Waller, two of Osseo's earliest residents of Norwegian heritage. Sadly, the historic building unexpectedly burned to the ground on January 4, 1989.

The next building after the Farmer's Store was a doctor's office where three doctors: Robert Leasum, Brad Garber and Richard Garber practiced medicine in the 1960s. Long before the building became a doctor's office though, it was the location of a bank that served the community. The above-mentioned medical group subsequently built a new clinic adjacent to the Osseo Area Municipal Hospital in the early 1970s, and since that time, the older building has served as home to several different businesses. For a time it also served as a modest apartment building. Interestingly enough, the safe that the old bank used is still there.

With the next block came Stub's Bar, one of Osseo's five drinking establishments in the downtown area. Directly behind Stub's Bar was Ozzie Borud's Television. Mr. Borud had a well-deserved reputation as being one of the slowest repairmen in the world. Still, if an old t.v. could be repaired, Ozzie knew how to do it; you just had to be ready to go without the television set for an extended time. Over the years, I was fortunate enough to get to know Ozzie Borud, and I found him to be a highly intelligent and kindhearted gentleman–but he really was the slowest repairman in the world. Beside Stub's Bar was the Osseo Post Office. The Post Office moved to a location along US Highway 53 several years later, but it was located on Seventh Street in 1967.

The next business on Seventh Street was the dental office of Dr. K. L. Herbert. His dental practice was only at that location for a brief time before he opened a modern dental office beside Lake Martha on US Highway 53. However, that was where he practiced dentistry when I moved to Osseo in 1967. Adjacent to the dental office was Speich's Pharmacy. I frequently picked up Ma's prescription medicines from that store. The last store on the block was an old-fashioned variety store called Carter's Dime Store. I purchased a lot of candy bars at Carter's as a kid. Later, when I was in junior high, I purchased more than a couple of friendship rings for the girls I went "steady" with at that store. Behind Carter's was a building referred to as the telephone company. We went on field trips to that business in grade school.

One block further east, on the north side of Seventh Street, was the printing press for Osseo's newspaper, a weekly publication called the Tri-County News. Years earlier the newspaper was called the Osseo News, and a variation of that name was what my mother used when referencing the publication. I remember well the way she pronounced the name. I might ask, "Whatcha reading Ma?" Ma would invariably reply, "Oh, the Osseo Snooze." Beside the printing office was an old garage where all of the school buses and other vehicles belonging to the school district received routine maintenance.

Below the city garage and printing office was a bowling alley that was officially called the Osseo Lanes. However, few of Osseo's residents referred to the establishment by its official name. Virtually everyone in Osseo referred to the place as the Hole. And while the other four drinking establishments located on or near Seventh Street catered to Osseo's older residents, the Hole catered to a younger, rowdier crowd of people. The name of the bar was changed from the Osseo Lanes to the Underground in the early 1970s, but the new name never caught on any more than the old name. People still called the place the Hole.

When the Osseo Lanes became the Underground, the bowling lanes were covered over so that the area could be converted into a dance floor. A barrier fence was also put in place to separate the dancing area from the bar. Although the official drinking age in Wisconsin in the 1970s was 18, the state was pretty relaxed about allowing underage people inside bars. That said, the bartenders at the Hole took things to another level altogether. In other words, they were as relaxed at checking for identification as a business could possibly be. Underage teenagers were authorized to enter the Hole to attend the dances held there, and once inside it was pretty easy to sneak over to the other side of the barrier, gradually straddle up to the bar and order a beer. I know that it was easy to do because I did it so many times when I was a teenager.

On the south side of Seventh Street, again going east from where it intersected with US Highway 53, stood the Corner Café, the first of two dining restaurants on Seventh Street, with the other one being the Star Café. I always preferred the burgers and fries at the Corner Café to those served at the Star Café, particularly after I became a teenager. That was because the person who owned the Corner Café allowed us to hang out at the restaurant. It wasn't at all uncommon to find seven or more teenagers sitting in the booths and smoking cigarettes while listening to music on the jukebox. Sadly, the Corner Café burned to the ground in May 1973.

Next to the Corner Café was a business known as Osseo Apparel and

Shoe. The establishment was owned by two businesswomen named Anne Hagen and Dorothy Bratsven. Mrs. Bratsven was the mother of a girl that I "liked" when I was a child. One day when my friend Don Keffer and I were shopping for our new school shoes, he innocently informed Mrs. Bratsven that I liked her daughter. I was embarrassed and angered by Donald's comment and as soon as we exited the store, I sucker punched him in the gut and yelled, "Damn it Donald, why did you tell her that?" Donald and I later worked the matter out and our friendship remained strong for years. However, I'm sure he was upset with me for quite some time for unexpectedly punching him.

Osseo Apparel and Shoe was eventually replaced by two businesses: Mike Sales Television occupied the eastern half and American Family Insurance occupied the western half. After Osseo Apparel and Shoe was the Star Café, the second of the two restaurants on Seventh Street. In 1973, the Star Café was purchased by a businesswoman named Helen Myhre. At that time the restaurant's name was changed to the Norske Nook, and the rest, as the saying goes, is history.

The Norske Nook almost immediately gained a highly favorable reputation throughout the Midwest for its homemade pies and Norwegian cultural theme. Lost on most people was the fact that pies have no particular cultural connection to Norway. Nobody cared! The pies served at the Norske Nook tasted delicious and that was why people from all over the area drove to Osseo to dine there. The pies served at the Norske Nook were so incredibly delicious that at one point, *Esquire* magazine named the Norske Nook as one of the 10 best restaurants in America.

A small fire broke out in the original Norske Nook in the early 1980s. My friend Cary Hagen was a member of Osseo's all-volunteer fire department at the time. Cary was home when the fire siren sounded, but he immediately started driving in the direction of the fire station. Along the way he passed by the restaurant and observed billows of smoke rising into the small apartment located above. Cary knew that an elderly individual lived inside that apartment, so he parked his car and rushed towards the upstairs apartment. When Carry arrived a few moments later, he found the elderly individual sleeping in his bed. In truly heroic fashion, Cary immediately woke the senior citizen up and escorted him out of the apartment and downstairs to safety.

A new and larger version of the restaurant was constructed on the north side of Seventh Street in 1994. Once the new restaurant was finished, the old restaurant was converted into a gift shop called the *Kaffe Hus og Gave Butikk,* or the Coffee House and Gift Boutique. However, when I moved to Osseo in 1967, the Norske Nook didn't exist and the Star Café was still located on the south side of Seventh Street. At the end of the block where the old Star Café stood was another business called the Gambles Store. I always thought the Gambles Store sold an interesting variety of products for one store. The products ranged from farming supplies to kitchen appliances to hunting gear and camping equipment. The Gambles Store was owned by two gentlemen named Chuck Rongstad and Mel Krienke.

When I was a 12-year-old, I enrolled in a hunter safety course that was taught by Chuck Rongstad. The course was sponsored by the National Rifle Association, and as strange as it may sound in today's world, my friends and I carried our rifles inside the school building to our assigned classroom one evening per week for the duration of the course. It is difficult to imagine teenagers receiving authorization to carry their rifles onto school grounds today for any reason–including hunter safety. However, nobody gave the matter a second thought in the City of Osseo in the early 1970s.

I purchased my first and second bikes at the Gambles Store. After I learned how to ride a bike, Ma purchased a handsome new bicycle for me: a red, 26-inch single-speed Huffy. The bike had a wide cross-bar with large front and rear chrome fenders and a built-in light in front. Unfortunately, the bike was stolen a short time after Ma purchased it for me. When Ma realized how sad I was, she took sympathy on my plight and bought a second bike. Specifically, a jet-black, 26-inch three-speed Hiawatha. After receiving the new Hiawatha, I felt as though I was riding on top of the world again.

At the beginning of the next block was Martin's Bar. The business was owned and operated by the parents of my friend Jody Martin. I spent a lot of time with Jody inside that bar when we were kids. We stopped there after school sometimes to have a bottle of Hires Root Beer and a bag of Old Dutch Potato Chips, always courtesy of Jody's parents. Jody and I were close friends throughout grade school and junior high. However, we eventually drifted apart. Jody dropped out of high school when he turned 16. Sadly, he was seriously hurt in a one-car automobile accident that occurred in Chippewa Falls, Wisconsin, on Friday, May 30, 1980.

The one-car accident happened shortly after midnight when Jody was driving to an industrial park to pick up a friend of his at the end of a shift. Jody was traveling east on First Avenue when his car crashed through some barricades and plunged into a 15 to 20 feet deep hole located at the intersection of First Avenue and Palmer Street. It is believed the accident happened around midnight. However, Jody wasn't spotted until the following morning around 6:30a.m. when several construction workers reported for work and discovered the wreckage. An ambulance was immediately called, but it took another 25 minutes for ambulance workers to extricate Jody from his vehicle.

Initially, the ambulance transported Jody to St. Joseph's Hospital in Chippewa Falls. However, due to the serious nature of his injuries, he was immediately transported to Sacred Heart Hospital in Eau Claire. He sustained head and chest injuries as well as a badly broken leg. Jody also lost a substantial amount of blood and suffered from hypothermia by the time he was placed inside the ambulance. I remember visiting him in the hospital the following day. He was in what a nurse described as a coma. His left arm was tied to his bed rail, but it kept involuntarily rotating in a circular motion. Also, his leg was in a cast. Perhaps the most frightening sight of all was looking into Jody's eyes. They were open, but not focused on any one thing in particular. Instead, they seemed to stare off into the distance as his head moved steadily about, but in no particular pattern.

Unfortunately, Jody Martin never fully recovered from his injuries. His broken leg healed, but he walked with a great deal of difficulty. His chest injuries also healed. However, the injuries to his brain were sufficiently serious that he was never able to fully function as an adult again. Jody lived with his parents in Osseo for a time. However, he was later admitted to an adult care facility in Eau Claire, Wisconsin, where he lived for several years. Jody's father passed away in 1985, and his mother passed away in 2007. Jody currently lives under the guardianship of one of his half-brothers in the western United States. I spoke to his half-brother on one occasion, and he informed me that Jody no longer remembers anything about Osseo or his old friends.

Returning now to Seventh Street, an attractive circular-shaped bank was constructed in an area directly behind Martin's Bar in June 1970. However, the previously described bank located on the north side of Seventh Street was still in operation when I moved to Osseo in 1967. Behind Martin's Bar was another building where two well-respected attorneys named John Ward and Richard Galstad practiced law for several years. Although they were part of a law firm based in Arcadia, Wisconsin, messrs. Galstad and Ward worked as partners in Osseo from 1957 until 1983, when Richard Galstad was appointed Trempealeau County Circuit Judge by the governor.

John Ward took on his most high-profile criminal case not long after I moved to Osseo in 1967. The remains of a man named Harry Melby were discovered to the west of Osseo on the north side US Highway 53 and US Highway 10, on Friday, September 22, 1967. A man who owned some land where County Road K connects with the highways named Ed Colvin was inspecting his lots when he discovered a wallet containing the driver's license of Harry Melby. Suspecting something wasn't right, Mr. Cloven immediately brought the wallet to the nearby home of Patrolman Harry Strong.

After examining the wallet and informing Ed Colvin that the police had been searching for Mr. Melby the past few days, they returned to the area where the wallet was found. A short time later, they found other items including a wristwatch band, a pair of eyeglasses and false teeth. When the additional items were found, Harry Strong called for additional assistance with the search. However, it was Ed Colvin who subsequently found Mr. Melby' remains. The badly beaten and partially decomposed body was located beneath some underbrush alongside the crumbling foundation of a once popular dance hall from the 1930s that was called the Nightingale Dance Pavilion.

Mr. Melby's head was discovered lying against part of the concrete foundation of the pavilion, about five feet away from a pile of rusted beer cans. Although the body wasn't discovered until September 22, subsequent investigation revealed that Harry Melby was murdered the previous Saturday, September 16. An autopsy conducted in the nearby City of Eau Claire determined the official cause of death was strangulation. Whoever murdered Harry Melby took the sleeve of his sport jacket and wrapped it around his throat. A stick was then used as a windlass to tighten the material around his throat in such a way as to choke him to death. The autopsy also found evidence of severe trauma throughout his upper body, as well as a broken jaw.

Harry Edwin Melby was born in the Town of Hale, near Pigeon Falls, Wisconsin, on March 3, 1890. Interestingly enough, his name at birth was Edward Sveum. When he was a young adult, Edward moved to St. Paul, Minnesota, where he found work as a streetcar conductor. Eventually, Edward met and married a woman named Pauline Seifert of Alma Center, Wisconsin. The couple had one child named Dorothy Pauline Sveum. However, their marriage ended in a divorce. Angry over the divorce and all that ensued, Edward Sveum had his name legally changed to Harry Melby and enlisted in the army.

Private First Class Harry Melby was severely wounded in France during World War I and received a Purple Heart. When the Great War ended, Harry Melby eventually settled in Osseo, where he soon found work as a shoe salesman and professional photographer. Harry Melby was living in an upstairs apartment above the Farmer's Store on Seventh Street at the time of his death. His funeral was held at the Osseo Evangelical Lutheran Church on Monday, September 25, 1967, with the Reverend LeRoy Johnsrud officiating. Harry Edwin Melby is buried at Pigeon Falls Evangelical Lutheran Cemetery.

After the murder, his friends described Harry Melby to the media as a quiet, unobtrusive individual who was no more than five feet seven inches tall. They also described him as a clean and neat individual who wore stylish clothing and frequently flashed a large diamond ring on his finger. He was also known to carry a large wad of cash on him at all times. Harry Melby was last seen alive at Martin's Bar located on Seventh Street on Saturday, September 16. Merle Andrus, an elderly man that I worked for and became friends with only a few years later, shared a few bottles of beer with Harry Melby that evening and was one of the last people to have seen him alive. At some point later that night Harry Melby had asked two young men, Douglas Fellenz, age 18, and Aaron Kotlarz, age 22, to give him a ride to the Chief Inn Supper Club, located a few miles west of Osseo.

Aaron Kotlarz was from Arcadia and Douglas Fellenz was from Blair. However, they both lived in Whitehall when they gave Harry Melby a ride. When the two suspects were subsequently questioned by law enforcement officials, they acknowledged giving Melby a ride to the Chief Inn Supper Club, but insisted the last time they saw him was when they dropped him off at the restaurant. However, none of the staff nor the patrons who were at the Chief Inn that night remembered seeing Harry Melby at the supper club. At the conclusion of the investigation, a determination was made to arrest both suspects.

Aaron Kotlarz was arrested at a hotel in Beaver Dam on Saturday,

September 23. Initially, he was taken into custody by Dodge County officials. He was brought to the Trempealeau County jail by Sheriff Eugene Bijold and a deputy named Alf Wilberg later that same day. Coincidentally, Douglas Fellenz was already confined at the Jail on other charges at the time of his arrest. Aaron Kotlarz was officially charged with first degree murder and robbery on September 29, and Doug Fellenz was formally charged with second-degree murder and robbery at the same time.

John O. Ward represented Aaron Kotlarz while an attorney from Gailsville represented Fellenz. As a testament to John Ward's skills as an attorney, he and the attorney representing Fellenz were able to negotiate reduced charges for both their defendants. After a series of difficult negotiations with Trempealeau County District Attorney William Matka, the charges were reduced from first-degree murder and robbery for Kotlarz, and second-degree murder and robbery for Fellenz, to third-degree murder and robbery for both defendants. The defendants subsequently pleaded guilty to the reduced charges on April 1, 1968. Judge Albert L. Twesme imposed sentence on both defendants on April 9, 1968.

Defendants Kotlarz and Fellenz both received 15-year sentences for their third-degree murder convictions and two-year sentences for the robbery convictions. The defendants might have received harsher sentences, but at the time they were sentenced, 15 years was the maximum sentence possible for a third-degree murder conviction in Wisconsin. The convicted felons were both ordered to serve their state sentences at what was then called the Green Bay Reformatory. The same prison is now called the Green Bay Correctional Institution. Convicted felon Douglas Fellenz was released from prison on January 15, 1979, and convicted felon Aaron Kotlarz was discharged from his sentence on October 15, 1981.

The next business after Martin's Bar on Seventh Street was Chase's Barber Shop, and then came One Hour Martinizing, a dry cleaning business. Next was the storefront for Eddie Barber's Electric, and that was followed by the Osseo Meat Locker. Hunters brought their deer there, and area farmers brought their hogs and cattle in to have the meat processed. Beside the Osseo Meat Locker was the Osseo Bakery, an establishment that was owned by the parents of my friend Robert Kershner. There were always fresh rolls, breads and a number of other pastries for sale at that bakery and it was all made by hand on a daily basis. I stayed overnight at Robert's house several times and remember how his parents, Russell and Alice, always got up early in the morning to go to work at their bakery. They had to prepare all of the fresh pastries and breads before opening for business. In the process, I got to know them very well. Russell passed away in 1988, and Alice passed away in 2004. They are buried beside one another at the Osseo Cemetery.

Robert and I remained good friends throughout our high school years, and our friendship continued for a time after he completed his first enlistment in the United States Army. However, we were never closer friends than we were in high school. Russell allowed Robert to drive his Monte Carlo, and I fondly remember the two of us cruising around the back roads in that car, drinking ice-cold beer, smoking cigarettes and listening to music. The last time I saw Robert Kershner was on Superbowl Sunday, January 25, 1981. He had just received an honorable discharge from the Army and lived in an apartment in Eau Claire. Sadly, we never had an opportunity to get together again. He passed away from cancer in 2021.

The last business on that block was Olson's Bar, another of the five drinking establishments located in the area. One block to the east, but still on the south side of Seventh Street was an old apartment building and a tiny building where the telephone company had once operated. After that was Vold's Implement, a highly successful farm implement business that sold new and used machinery. My brother Irvin worked at Vold's for several years as a mechanic making repairs to farm machinery. I was always impressed by the almost trance-like state that the mechanics fell into while working at their craft. He once described to me that he tried to think like the machine in an effort to better understand how the machine he was working on was supposed to operate. Then, after identifying what had to be done to restore the machine to working order, Irvin made the necessary repairs. Vold's Implement moved from its location on Seventh Street to a location near Interstate 94 at some point in 1976.

The last two businesses on Seventh Street were located where things transitioned from a traditional business district into a residential area. Those two businesses were the Oftedahl Funeral Home and Dr. Oris Idsvoog's Veterinary Clinic. I had attended Pappy's and Ma's wake inside the funeral home, but never stepped inside the veterinary clinic. A student in my class named Barbara was Dr. Idsvoog's daughter. We were never close friends. Nevertheless, I've always had a special place for her in my heart, and that is because her father was killed in an automobile accident one week to the day after my brother Freddie was killed in an automobile accident. Dr. Idsvoog was killed on August 12, 1967. He was a respected member of the community who owned and operated a highly successful veterinary practice in Osseo. Dr. Oris Idsvoog and two others were killed when their vehicles collided in what officials described as one of the worst automobile accidents in Osseo's history.

The accident occurred at the intersection of what was State Highway 27 and US Highway 10, but is now County Road R and US Highway 10. The 47-year-old Dr. Idsvoog was en route to an area farm where he had been summoned to provide veterinary care to a farm animal. Meanwhile, the 25-year-old Louis Ansorge, Jr., and his 24-year-old wife Sandra Orthober Ansorge, were passing through the area on their way to Alaska, where they were about to begin a two year teaching assignment at Clark's Point. Their two-year-old daughter Ligeia was traveling with them when the accident happened.

Louis Ansorge was from Manitowoc, Wisconsin, and his wife Sandra was from Menomonee Falls, Wisconsin. She was pronounced dead at the Osseo Area Municipal Hospital at 2:30p.m. and her husband was pronounced dead approximately one hour later. Fortunately, their two-year-old daughter escaped serious injuries. She was eventually placed in the custody of her paternal grandparents, Louis and Lucille Ansorge of Manitowoc. Dr. Idsvoog was committed to Rest Haven Gardens in Eau Claire. Louis and Sandra Ansorge were laid to rest at Knollwood Memorial Gardens in Manitowoc.

After spending a considerable amount of time walking up and down Seventh Street and thinking back on times spent there, I decided to drive over to one of Osseo's newer drinking establishments, a popular bar called the Northwoods Brew Pub. The bar was built inside the previously-described building called the condensery. I had only been inside the pub once but remembered it as a warm and inviting bar. Fortunately, nothing had changed. After ordering a can of Walter's beer I sat down on a barstool and enjoyed the beverage. As I relaxed in those handsome surroundings, I began reflecting back on my adolescence.

TEENAGE WILDLIFE

Although I always felt content spending time alone as a teenager, I truly enjoyed being in the company of others. However, I generally preferred hanging around with one or two friends at most. Other than time spent around family members, large groups of people usually seemed a lot less enjoyable than small groups of one or two people. As a teenager, I did almost everything with a certain friend for a time. Then, I invariably drifted toward other interests, and whenever that happened, a new friend supplanted the previous friend, at least for a time. Drifting in and out of friendships in this way was fluid, and the person I hung out with one summer might well be the person I hung out with the following winter. However, I might have spent little or no time with them throughout the intervening autumn.

As previously stated, my very first friend was a boy was Brian Maug. However, after moving to Osseo, I became friends with several other kids including Donald Keffer. He and I spent a lot of time together riding our bikes around. One time we rode them a few miles into the country to the home of a girl named Joanne Frase. Don had a crush on her at the time and explained to me that he just had to see her. The experience was a lot more enjoyable for Don than it was for me. After we finally arrived at Joanne's home, Donald gave his undivided attention to Joanne and I became the odd person out. The two of them snuck off together and started making out while I sat and twiddled my thumbs until it was time to ride our bikes back to Osseo.

Another kid I made friends with was named Del Van Blaricom. We first met in the sixth grade and hit it off right away, remaining close to one another throughout our junior high school and high school years. Sometimes we hung out together in a wooded area behind his house. The North Fork Buffalo River passed directly behind the house his mother rented, and within that wooded area was a small island we named Coconut Island. There were no coconut trees there of course, but that's the name we gave the tiny island. Del had a younger sister nicknamed Coco, and I suspect the name Coconut Island came to us after hearing her nickname a one point. At any rate, someone cut a large tree down in those woods and the felled tree connected Coconut Island to the surrounding woods. Del and I usually killed time there on weekends before going to a Sage Dance at the City Hall Building or a sporting event at the high school.

By the time I entered the topsy-turvy world of junior high school, an overwhelming interest in girls had taken over much of my thinking. So did my curiosity about what was going on around Osseo after sundown. However, to experience first hand that which occurred after the sun went down, I had to be out and about at night. That meant I had to come up with a means of sneaking out of Ma's place to see for myself exactly what was going on. I remember thinking it was a significant personal accomplishment when I learned how to crawl over the railing surrounding the balcony atop the entryway to Ma's place and hang over the side. At first, that was about as far as I took the challenge, and after hanging from the side of the balcony for a while, I crawled back onto the balcony and went inside the house.

Not long after becoming a teenager though, I started jumping off the side of the balcony to the ground below. I fell hard the first few times, but it became easier over time and eventually I was jumping off the side of the balcony with ease. I also learned how to crawl back up the side of the entryway, step over the balcony railing and go inside the house again. That was my primary means of sneaking out and getting back inside Ma's place when I was a teenager. One of the places that I frequently went after sneaking out of Ma's place was Stoddard Park.

Near to the eastern edge of the park–not very far from the wooden footbridges referenced earlier–stood a handsome one-room log cabin. The log cabin was built there so that golfers could stop and rest while playing a round of golf at Osseo's impressive nine-hole golf course. By the early 1970s, that log cabin had become a hangout where some of my friends and I spent time shooting the breeze prior to attending various events in the community.

As I recall, my friend and I enjoyed spending time at the cabin and thought of it as a place where we could interact without too much unwanted interference from adults. Sure, a drunk golfer might shout profanities at us from time to time as he approached the teeing ground with his fellow golfers, but whenever that happened we just scurried off for a few minutes. Then, once the complaining golfers teed off and proceeded on their way, we returned to the cabin and continued whatever it was that we were doing before the unwelcome intrusion.

One of the girls I spent time with at that one-room cabin was named Julie Johnson. She lived in the country with her parents in a house located on Johnson Road near the community of Foster Wisconsin. The students living in Foster began attending school at Osseo in the seventh grade. I fell hard for Julie as soon as I saw her on our first day of junior high and fortunately, she felt the same way about me. Julie was kind of shy, but she was also attractive and I sincerely cared for her. Julie was also a well-endowed girl, and in all honesty, I was as attracted to her for that reason as I was to her friendly personality.

> *She's so naive and innocent, stares at you with awe*
> *She's only fourteen, but she knows how to draw*
> *Donovan*

As with the majority of the students in our school, Julie's parents were Lutherans, and they enrolled her in confirmation classes in Osseo, even though there was a Lutheran church in Foster. However, the church in Foster was a Lutheran Church Missouri Synod (LCMS) church, and her parents, Ruth and Maurice "Kooga" Johnson, were of the opinion that the LCMS church adhered to a number of rules and customs that were sufficiently different for them to worship at the American Lutheran Church Synod (ALC) church located in Osseo. Our confirmation classes were held on Thursday evenings. So, rather than ride the bus back to her parents' place on the outskirts of Foster after school, Julie stayed in Osseo. Unfortunately, after Julie and I entered high school, we gradually drifted apart and I did not speak to her until roughly 2010. Julie (Brackin) passed away from cancer in Cochrane, Wisconsin, in 2017.

From as far back as my move to Osseo in 1967, I've usually had a part-time or full-time job of one kind or another that always kept me in spending money. As a result, I spent my youth and adolescence without want for any material things. The first job I had was selling Christmas cards to people living in Osseo. It wasn't a traditional job in that I didn't receive a paid hourly wage nor a commission. Instead, I earned prizes based on how many Christmas cards I sold to people. There was a company that operated out of White Plains, New York, that encouraged kids to sell different kinds of cards to people. I took them up on their offer and started selling Christmas cards to people around Osseo. The company mailed a catalog to me that contained samples of the various cards available. I then went door-to-door with those samples, asking people if they wanted to purchase a box or two of the cards from me.

For whatever reason, I was very good at selling Christmas cards. It may have been the novelty of my riding up to houses on my bike–in the dead of summer–and presenting the people who lived there with colorful examples of all those pretty Christmas cards that made me so successful. Perhaps it was the quality of the cards alone that made me successful. I don't know. What I do know is that I managed to sell a lot of Christmas cards when I was a kid, and in turn I received a lot of nice prizes that included my first acoustic guitar, my first camping tent and my first sleeping bag. The prizes were all top-quality items too, and I can honestly say that I was pleased with everything that I selected.

Another job I had was working for my brother Irvin on his tiny dairy farm. Usually, I worked for him on weekends, but I worked full-time during haying season. Irvin picked me up in his pick-up truck at Ma's place and brought me to his farm near the unincorporated community of Foster. While working for him, I quickly learned the meaning of the word thrifty. Irvin wouldn't allow anything to go to waste. After his corn was harvested from the field, Irvin handed a bushel basket to me and told me to go into the field and pick up the cobs of corn that had been left behind by the corn picker! I remember walking up and down the already harvested rows of corn stocks while holding that bushel basket and picking up the cobs of corn that had dropped on the ground. I then tossed the bushel baskets of gathered cobs into the back of his pickup, which he had parked in the middle of the field. As if yesterday, I remember that my always "thrifty" brother paid me $2.00 a day in wages. Not $2.00 an hour, but $2.00 a day in wages.

When Irvin and his wife Nola purchased their farm, the fences were in bad shape, so we installed new barbed wire fencing throughout his entire farm. The job involved manually digging countless post holes for wooden posts as well as manually driving steel fence posts into the ground. Irvin did the hardest work by digging most of the post holes and driving in most of the steel fence posts. I primarily assisted him by putting new posts in the ground and filling in the dirt around them. Once the fence posts were firmly in place, we worked together to string the barbed wire along the fence line and then fasten the wire to the posts.

What I remember most fondly about the time I spent working for Irvin was the time that we constructed a milk house inside his dairy barn. It was my first experience with construction, and I found the process fascinating. We ran the water lines and did the electrical work ourselves. We also poured the concrete, laid anchor bolts and assembled the walls and ceiling. The milk house served Irvin well for several years until he replaced all of his older outbuildings, including the dairy barn, with new structures.

Most of the jobs I secured were part of a federal program called the

National Youth Corps that provided employment to low-income kids. I never saw myself as poor when I was growing up, and neither did my mother or siblings. And yet, by federal government standards, my family was deemed as having an annual income that fell well below the recognized poverty line. So, when the federal government began the work program during the Nixon administration, I quickly applied for a job. For the above-stated reasons I was consistently selected for employment through the National Youth Corps program, and worked at those jobs throughout my junior high and high school years. One summer I was given a job as a groundskeeper at the local nine-hole golf course. Most of the summer was spent expanding a previously undeveloped area of the golf course by cutting down and removing a stand of woods and underbrush. I used a handheld saw and sickle to cut back all of the underbrush before carrying it away.

I had other, easier assignments as well, such as moving the holes on the putting greens once a week. It was also my job to pour chemicals into the pond every week to keep the water free of algae. I also raked the sand traps every day to ensure that the sand was evenly spread about. Without raking the sand, it tended to drift toward the bottom. By doing those and other jobs, I became familiar with the layout of the entire golf course. However, I never played a single game of golf at the attractive course. Quite candidly, I never developed an interest in the sport or the people who found golf an enjoyable activity.

My favorite job with the National Youth Corps involved working as a custodian at the high school. The crew of janitors I worked for was supervised by a hard-nosed individual named Chet Lien. However, the janitor I routinely worked for was a kind gentleman named Larry Gomsrud. As with most places throughout the United States I think, the janitors at the Osseo-Fairchild High School took a lot of breaks during the work day, so I did as well. Those breaks were particularly enjoyable whenever I had a chance to listen to the two most elderly janitors: Merle Andrus and Millard Davidson, engage in conversation. Merle told the wildest stories about serving as a soldier in the Pacific theater during World War II. Millard was essentially his sidekick and always laughed at the stories–no matter how many times he had heard them before. Millard and Merle were an entertaining couple to listen to and I enjoyed their company very much.

From the money I earned at various jobs I had, I was able to purchase virtually every piece of camping equipment that a teenager needed to go camping in relative comfort. I loved sleeping outdoors and going camping more than just about anything else when I was a teenager, and I did so as frequently as possible. I enjoyed doing so, both in the City of Osseo and out in the country. More often than not that meant camping at the Rod and Gun Club located a couple of miles south of Osseo off US Highway 53. The Rod and Gun Club was formed in 1890 and was routinely used by several of Osseo's residents. I never hunted or engaged in activities such as target practice at the Rod and Gun Club. However, I spent a lot of time fishing along the shore of the seven acre man-made pond located there.

When I was a youth, I sometimes went camping there with my friend Craig Indrebo. However, in junior high and high school I camped with others as well. The camping trips consisted mostly of eating, hiking, eating, talking, eating, fishing, eating, sleeping and more eating! Needless to say, we spent a lot of time sitting around our campfires preparing, cooking and consuming a lot of food. The food was always prepared over an open fire too. Propane stoves weren't considered an option in those days. When we weren't eating we went on leisurely hikes along the area's many well-worn paths.

We also spent time fishing at the man-made pond that was supposedly stocked with good-sized trout. My friend Craig Indrebo and I fished side-by-side along the shore of the pond. He managed to catch some of those trout every time we went fishing. However, I wasn't quite as lucky. In fact, the only kind of fish I remember catching at the Rod and Gun Club were tiny panfish. Although the fishing at the Rod and Gun Club may have left a lot to be desired, my friends and I enjoyed casting our lines into the water before sitting back and shooting the breeze while waiting for those elusive trophy-sized trout to take a bite at the bait. It didn't seem to matter very much that they seldom did.

When my friends and I weren't camping out at the Rod and Gun Club, we were swimming at the municipal swimming pool, chasing girls or holding boxing matches. As alluded to earlier, most of the boxing matches that I arranged were held in the garden at my friend Robert Kershner's house, a location that we referred to as Kershner's Square Garden. However, not all of the boxing matches were held there. I arranged the boxing matches that were held in wintertime down in the basement at Ma's place. Unquestionably, the best and most competitive boxing match I arranged was the one between Jody Martin and Wendell Pederson.

Wendell lived on a dairy farm on County Road E, halfway between Osseo and the unincorporated community of Pleasantville. As a kid living on a large dairy farm, Wendell had a lot of heavy manual work to complete every day, and that gave him a lot of physical strength. But Wendell wasn't only strong, he was also incredibly athletic and had been that way throughout his grade school and junior high years. That wasn't the case for Jody Martin, who was overweight, even flabby throughout his grade school years. Jody hadn't really been thought of as either strong or athletic as a kid. However, that all changed when he went through puberty. It seemed that almost overnight he lost all of his excess weight and replaced it with solid muscle.

Desperately wanting to prove to his classmates that he was no longer the pudgy kid from grade school that everybody knew, Jody jumped at the opportunity to fight a popular, athletic kid such as Wendell. Because Wendell had always been supremely self-confident in his athletic abilities, he enthusiastically agreed to fight Jody. As I recall, there were at least five or six people present to watch the fight in the basement. Donald Keffer served as Wendell Pederson's corner man and Robert Kershner served in that same capacity as Jody Martin's assistant. I was the referee.

When the bell rang for the first round, it was immediately clear to me that Wendell had gotten inside Jody's head. For the first two minutes of the fight, Jody stood frozen in the center of the ring while Wendell pummeled him with jab after jab after jab. Fortunately, by the second round Jody seemed to have found his mojo, and began throwing a few powerful punches at Wendell–with a couple of them landing squarely on the jaw. Still, for every punch Jody successfully landed, Wendell countered with several quick, stinging jabs. Soon Jody's ordinarily pale face appeared flushed and his eyes were beginning to swell shut.

As Jody's frustration grew, he inexplicably began putting his tongue between his teeth while grimacing. By the start of the fifth round, it was clear that Wendell was going to win the seven-round bout by a unanimous decision, and that was what everyone expected. However, just before the sixth round came to a close, Wendell threw a powerful uppercut that caught Jody squarely on the chin. The punch didn't knock Jody out–or even knock him down. What the uppercut did do was violently force Jody's teeth to close, nearly severing his tongue in the process. With a lot of blood dripping from his mouth, and pain undoubtedly shooting through his tongue, Jody put his hands in the air and said, "Forget it man! I'm done with this shit!" That was it, I blew my whistle and yelled, "The fight is over!" Then I grabbed hold of Wendell's arm and raised it into the air, signaling to everyone that he had won the fight.

As I sat inside the Northwoods Brew Pub drinking my beer, I was reminded of another experience with Jody Martin. When we were 14-year-olds, Jody, Del Van Blaricom and I decided to build a fort in a stand of woods located only a short distance from where I was enjoying my beer. Back then, though, the building was still the abandoned condensery. While hiking around in the area one day, we discovered what looked like a pile of abandoned lumber. At 14 we should have known the boards belonged to somebody. However, we helped ourselves to all of the lumber we wanted from the pile and constructed two good-sized forts. Throughout the rest of the summer, Del, Jody and I frequently camped out inside those forts. We didn't think much about who that lumber belonged to at the time. However, in hindsight it seems likely it belonged to Gordon Hong, the owner of the nearby Hong Lumber Company.

At the southern edge of Stoddard Park, was a nine-hole golf course and next to the golf course was a bar and restaurant called the Osseo Country Club. Adjacent to the Country Club was a good-sized paved area where the annual Labor Day Celebration was held. Most of the small cities and towns in west central Wisconsin held an annual fair of one kind or another. The City of Arcadia held a Broiler Festival and the City of Whitehall sponsored an event called Beef and Dairy Days. The City of Augusta put on its annual Bean and Bacon Days and the City of Alma Center held an event called the Strawberry Festival. The Village of Strum held an event called Strum Steam Engine Days, and the City of Blair held an annual Cheese Festival.

The Labor Day Celebration was tiny by any measure. At most there were five rides for teenagers and adults and three or four rides for little children. Apart from the rides, there were concession stands that offered cotton candy and caramel apples, etcetera. There were also a small number of booths where people tried to win prizes by throwing darts at balloons, shooting air guns at targets or tossing balls through hoops, etcetera. As has always been the case with carnival events throughout the United States, I suspect most of the games at the Labor Day Celebration in Osseo were rigged. However, just enough people succeeded in winning prizes to tempt other attendees into trying their luck at winning a teddy bear or some similar prize for their loved one.

The annual Labor Day Celebration was my favorite time of year. As a kid I always enjoyed going on the rides and eating the food, etcetera. However, as a teenager I came to appreciate the event for a number of different reasons; the Labor Day Celebration was a time to act cool while walking around with my friends from Osseo and Fairchild. I remember feeling especially fortunate on the nights when I was lucky enough to hold a girl's hand while we walked around the fairgrounds. The September nights were almost always chilly, so I usually wore a faded blue jean jacket over the shirt I had on, and that made me feel pretty cool as well.

I remember the colored lights on the concessions and rides as though I experienced them only yesterday. The spinning lights seemed to have a hypnotic effect on me, and I tried to be there to enjoy every minute of every evening that the fair was in Osseo. Eventually, the City of Osseo replaced the Labor Day Celebration with a new event called Lake Martha Days. However, that happened in 1981, well after I moved away from Osseo. I've never attended a Lake Martha Days celebration. Accordingly, I still think of the Labor Day Celebration as the annual event that brought the bright lights to the City of Osseo.

Yes, to dance beneath the diamond sky
With one hand waving free
Silhouetted by the sea
Circled by the circus sands
With all memory and fate, driven deep beneath the waves
Let me forget about today until tomorrow

Bob Dylan

The school year at Osseo-Fairchild High School usually began the last week in August. However, the annual Labor Day Celebration arrived the first week in September, and that meant we had one last long and entertaining weekend of fun and mischief before seriously settling in at school and hitting the books. Sadly, the Labor Day weekend of my sophomore year ended with anything but feelings of fun and festivity. A former student named Frederick Carl Fischer was killed in a two-vehicle, head-on collision on Tuesday, September 3, 1974. A woman named Judith "Judy" Herrick, age 32, was also killed in the accident. Freddie was only eighteen at the time of his death, and had graduated from high school the previous spring.

Freddie was driving his vehicle and Judy was a passenger in another vehicle driven by a man named Sydney Welter. The fatal automobile accident occurred southwest of Osseo at the crest of a hill on County Road H in Trempealeau County. Other passengers in the vehicles were Tom Maug, Doug Karlstad, Curt Monson and Yelanda Ray. Due to the serious nature of their injuries, Sydney Welter and Doug Karlstad were immediately transported to the Intensive Care Unit at Sacred Heart Hospital in Eau Claire. Sydney Welter received several lacerations, contusions and a concussion. Doug Karlstad sustained a fractured jaw, lacerations and a concussion. The other passengers were taken to the Osseo Area Municipal Hospital for their treatment. Judith Herrick is buried at the Osseo Cemetery. Freddie Fischer was laid to rest at the Hale Lutheran Cemetery.

When Del Van Blaricom and I were sophomores in high school, we started hanging out with an interesting individual named Martin Krenz. He was three years older than us and had graduated from high school, but we became good friends nevertheless. Martin was highly intelligent. More importantly, he was polite, considerate and always tolerant of others, personal qualities that made him the kind of person I felt proud to call my friend. One of the things we enjoyed doing together was go cruising around on the back roads surrounding Osseo. The car that Martin owned at the time was a truly distinctive 1950 Plymouth Special Deluxe. Whenever we went cruising around together, we always had a six-pack or 12-pack of beer in the backseat of Martin's Plymouth.

One of the reasons I liked Martin was that he was knowledgeable on a wide variety of subjects and it seemed that no matter what we talked about, he had an informed opinion. He was certainly more informed than I was on any given subject in those days. What I liked best about

Martin though, was the fact that he never tried to change my point of view. He seemed content in the correctness of his position and had little or no interest in arguing with others who might have a different opinion or point of view on any given subject.

One weekend while Martin, his brother Kenny, my friend Del and I were out cruising on County Road H, the same stretch of county road where Freddie Fischer had been killed, we observed a strange light in the sky. After spotting the light, I asked Martin to pull the Plymouth over to the side of the road so that we could get a better look. How I remember the incident is that once everybody stepped outside the car and looked up, we observed a bright light in the night sky. Using a combination of *Star Wars* and *Star Trek* terminology, we agreed that what we were observing was some kind of powerful laser or a tractor beam that was shooting down from a bright light that was hovering overhead. The sky was cloudy that night, and that made it appear as though the bright light appeared from behind the clouds.

We were slightly inebriated at the time, and in hindsight, I strongly suspect that helped convince us that we were looking at some kind of unidentified flying object hovering overhead in the night sky. Martin may have been a bit more skeptical than I was about what it was we were observing, but I nevertheless managed to convince him that we had to return to Osseo right away and report the matter to the police. After observing the powerful beam dart back and forth in the sky for a few more minutes, and no doubt arguing over what we should do, we finally got back inside Martin's Plymouth Special Deluxe and drove back to Osseo.

It just so happened that my brother-in-law, Wayne Holte, was the Sheriff of Trempealeau County at the time. Quite by chance, I had observed him and my sister Virginia walking into the Oasis Bar earlier that evening. So, as soon as we arrived in Osseo, I asked Martin to drive directly to the Oasis Bar. At that time we jumped out of the car and I walked inside the Oasis to tell Sheriff Holte what it was that we had witnessed above us in the sky. I strongly suspect the only reason my brother-in-law agreed to follow us out to the location of the "phenomena" we had observed was the fact that he was married to my sister Virginia. Regardless of the reason, Sheriff Holte agreed to follow us so that he could have a look at what we had seen.

Fortunately, the bright light and suspected tractor beam or laser were still visible in the sky when we returned to our previous location. We all got out of our vehicles and looked up at what we were convinced was an alien spacecraft. It took Sheriff Holte less than one minute to determine what it was that we were observing: a beacon light from a new business that had opened somewhere close by. The beacon light was used to capture the attention of passersby in an attempt to draw them to the location of the new business. After he explained the situation to us, Sheriff Holte gave us a look that said all that had to be said. We felt as embarrassed as hell as he drove away. However, Martin attempted to put a positive spin on the situation by telling us that it was our civic duty to report the matter to the authorities.

The first car I purchased was a light green 1966 Chevrolet Impala. I purchased the car from my sister Gloria for the whopping sum of $325.00. Ma thought Gloria had charged me too much money for the car. I respectfully disagreed. The Impala was a two-door hardtop with vinyl bucket seats and a four-speed manual transmission with positive traction and dual exhaust. Underneath the hood was a 327 cubic inch V-8 engine with a four barrel carburetor. The Impala was as close to a muscle car as any of the cars my friends drove. Sadly, the car had been poorly maintained for years and never ran well. One of its many faults was that it didn't have a reverse gear. Although I enjoyed the Impala and had a lot of truly memorable experiences driving around with my friends in it, I eventually grew tired of the frequent breakdowns and expenses that came with its maintenance.

In time I sold the Impala to another high school student named Jon Rongstad. However, before that transaction was made, my friends and I spent a considerable amount of time cruising around the back roads smoking cigarettes, drinking beer and listening to a lot of good music. One weekend in particular, my friend Brian Maug and I were cruising around in the Impala, when we heard that a beer party was going to be held later that night at an old abandoned house that was known to some of the teenagers around Osseo as Emma Bjerke's place. The property was located on an unnamed dirt road now called Ridge Lane.

Brian and I were familiar with the place inasmuch as we spent a lot of time playing there together when we were kids. Brian's parents were my sister Dorothy and a gentleman named Floyd Maug. They once lived on a small dairy farm located about five miles southeast of Osseo, off County Road E. Emma Bjerke's place was situated within walking distance from their dairy farm. Whenever I stayed overnight at Brian's farm, we went exploring inside Emma Bjerke's place. Due in part to our familiarity with the old abandoned building, and in part because of it's proximity to the farm where Brian once lived, we decided to go to the beer party that night.

Emma Bjerke's place had been a popular location for teenagers to hold beer parties for several years. And yet, in spite of the old abandoned house's notoriety amongst Osseo's teenagers, very few people knew anything about the individual who once lived there that everyone referred to as Emma Bjerke. In truth, the elderly woman was one of Osseo's invisible poor: an impoverished individual who was largely ignored and even shunned by most of Osseo's residents. Emma Bjerke was born on June 13, 1901. As an approximately 19-year-old woman, she married an elderly individual named Johanne Ellifson, who was 34 years older than Emma. The May-December couple were married around 1920. Unfortunately, Johanne Ellifson passed away in 1956 when Emma was approximately 55 years old. Emma passed away in 1974 when she was 72 years old.

Although Emma Ellifson had been living at the Osseo Area Nursing

Home at the time of her death, she previously spent several years at a mental health facility called the Trempealeau County Farm. This facility is now known as the Trempealeau County Health Care Center. After the death of her husband in 1956, but prior to her admission to the mental health facility in the nearby City of Whitehall, Wisconsin, Emma Ellifson lived a solitary life that can accurately be described as lonely and destitute. During wintertime, Emma sometimes stopped at my sister Dorothy's house to warm up over a cup or two of hot coffee. Other times, when the Maug family wasn't home, she helped herself to a bundle of their firewood and carried it back to her house.

Emma Ellifson had very few friends throughout her life, and her only known companionship came from the large clowder of cats that lived with her inside her house. Emma was so closely associated with her cats that some of Osseo's residents referred to her as "The Cat Lady" rather than by her name or Mrs. Ellifson. During the difficult years that Emma lived alone after her husbands death, she was frequently observed walking the roughly five mile distance to the City of Osseo. For several years she and her husband Johanne had walked that same route for the purpose of selling a few eggs as a means of earning a dollar or two in cash.

In latter years, Emma sometimes walked to Osseo in search of food and other handouts. Occasionally, a compassionate individual driving along the highway stopped and offered her a ride to town. However, most of the time she walked to Osseo alone, and after completing her business, walked the five miles back to her home alone. Fortunately, when the weather outside was particularly harsh, Patrolman Harry Strong, Osseo's one-armed police officer, was known to offer her a ride back to her house. However, most of the time Emma was left to make her own way home again on her own, virtually unnoticed by those passing by.

It wasn't long after Emma Ellifson was admitted to the Trempealeau County Farm, when her house was abandoned, that some of Osseo's teenagers began throwing beer parties there. At one point in the late 1960s, a group of particularly creative individuals that included a person named Dave Gilbertson initiated what came to be referred to as "The Great Ghost Hoax." Several years later, after I became friends with Dave, he shared some stories with me about Emma's place. First, he pointed out that there were a number of small, rolling hills located in the immediate vicinity of Emma Bjerke's place. Then he added that he and his friends took advantage of that hilly terrain when developing a clever stunt that made it appear to everyone attending the parties as though the ghost of Emma Bjerke suddenly appeared, before disappearing just as quickly into the darkness.

Another teenager involved with the pranking was particularly adapt at using electronics and that allowed the participants to incorporate a number of sound effects into the stunt as well. In hindsight, it seems highly unlikely that anyone present at those parties was fooled into believing they observed the ghost of Emma Bjerke in the distance. In reality, what the teenage partiers heard and witnessed was Dave and his friends dressed in a ghostly costume, briefly appearing on top of a hill before darting down into a low-lying area. Greatly embellished stories about the hoax undoubtedly contributed to the growing belief among some of Osseo's teenagers that Emma Bjerke's specter still dwelled within her old abandoned house.

A second event that added to the legend, and made Emma Bjerke's place an even more desirable location for underage beer parties, happened shortly after she was admitted to the Trempealeau County Farm. An individual named Christopher Hagen and one of his friends once rode their bicycles out to Emma Bjerke's place. Later in life, when I became friends with Christopher, he explained to me that almost immediately after his friend opened the door and walked inside the house he shouted, "Oh shit!" and ran back outside again. He continued running until he was a good distance from the house. Not really knowing why his friend had run away from the house, Christopher followed him.

After the teenagers were a good distance away from Emma Bjerke's place they stopped to catch their breath. Christopher then asked his friend why he had run away. In response, the visibly frightened teenager said he had seen a jar with human flesh inside on a shelf inside the house. At that time, Christopher and his friend rushed over to their bikes, got on them and rode back to Osseo as quickly as possible. In hindsight, is seems probable that when Emma Ellifson was removed from her home and admitted to the Trempealeau County Farm, she had to leave some of her belongings behind, including a jar of pickled pigs feet or some similar type of canned meat. Regardless of how implausible the story might have been, increasingly outlandish versions of their experience quickly spread around the City of Osseo and they also added to the legend that Emma Bjerke's place was a haunted house.

The beer party that Brian and I attended turned out to be pretty much the same as all of the other underage beer parties that were held around Osseo in those days. Everyone chipped in as much cash as possible, until there was enough money to purchase a keg of beer. Then someone asked an adult to purchase a quarter barrel or half barrel of beer, several bags of ice and some plastic drinking cups from a bar. A tap always had to be rented at the same time. Once the keg was delivered to Emma Bjerke's place, someone either twisted or slid the tap into place on top of the keg and secured it with a coupler. Then everyone got in line and started filling their plastic cups with beer. Those of us present that night continued drinking until the beer was gone.

It's probably safe to say that everyone attending the beer party was hoping to experience some type of paranormal activity that night. However, nothing out of the ordinary happened. Dave Gilbertson had long since moved away. In fact, by that time he had earned a Masters Degree in psychology and was working full-time at a mental health clinic in Port Huron, Michigan. After Dave and his generation of friends moved away, the tradition of organizing stunts similar to the previously described hoax fell out of favor. Instead, everyone present at the parties seemed content to stand around and shoot the breeze with their friends while drinking beer.

Unbeknownst to me at the time, Christopher Hagen was living inside the same farmhouse that Brian Maug lived in when he was a child. As such, he was more familiar than most with the history of Emma Bjerke's place. When Christopher and I became friends several years later, I asked him whatever happened to the house where Emma Bjerke once lived. Sadly, he informed me the house had been torn down and there was nothing left of the building. It came as no major surprise to me to learn that the house was gone. However, I was somewhat surprised to learn that a new house was constructed on the property as recently as the 2000s. Although Emma Bjerke's place no longer exists, it has been said that an old abandoned well still remains somewhere on the property, and that the well contains a number of artifacts that once belonged to Emma and Johanne Ellifson. Today, I "choose" to believe that story is true, and to preserve the veracity of the narrative, I have vowed to never search for that abandoned well....

Having learned that Emma Bjerke's place no longer exists, I began wondering what happened to Johanne and Emma Ellifson. I quickly discovered they are buried beside one another at the Hale Lutheran Cemetery, located approximately eight miles southeast of Osseo. Unfortunately, I also learned that some of the indignities the couple endured throughout their desperate lives continued after their deaths. When Emma passed away in 1972, the only thing that was placed on her gravesite was a small marker that was similar in size to the marker that had been placed on Johanne's grave years earlier. Apparently, there was insufficient funding available for the purchase of any type of permanent monument at the time of her death.

At some point after Johanne's burial, his marker was damaged by a lawnmower and removed from the gravesite. Still later, the marker which identified Emma's final resting place was removed by one or more unknown individuals. I was ultimately pleased to learn that a distant relative of Johanne and Emma Ellifson had recently purchased a granite memorial for the couple. The impressive slant monument was installed at the Hale Lutheran Cemetery as recently as the spring of 2022. When I learned that the memorial had been installed, I felt a subdued kind of personal satisfaction. It occurred to me that the impressive monument honored Johanne Ellifson and Emma (Bjerke) Ellifson with greater dignity in death than the frequently shunned couple had ever received during their difficult, impoverished lives.

The burden of someone else is always light
Norwegian Proverb

Almost immediately after I sold the Impala, I purchased a 1971 Ford Pinto hatchback. Talk about going from one extreme to another. The Pinto, along with American Motor Company's Gremlin, Dodge's Colt and Chevrolet's Vega, made up the first generation of American made four-cylinder economy cars. Suffice it to say that as a first-generation economy car, the Pinto was not a well-built machine. The car was small, sluggish, and generally boring to drive. Nevertheless, the car was reliable and affordable, which was more than could be said about the Impala.

After I purchased the Ford Pinto, I "souped" it up as best as I could by adding a set of chrome wheels, wide white wall tires and metallic mud flaps. I also mounted a chrome knob on the shifter. One of the more humorous modifications I made to the Pinto was replacing the factory muffler with one designed for use on Farmall M tractors. The muffler gave the Ford Pinto's four-cylinder engine a roar that, with a little imagination, sounded like a sports car. I also installed a top-of-the-line Pioneer car stereo with Jensen speakers. When all is said and done though, a lamb in wolf's clothing is still a lamb, and my Ford Pinto was nothing more than a "souped" up lamb of a car.

One of the people I hung around with in high school was John "Yogi"

Back. One of the reasons I liked him was that I thought he was the funniest person I had ever known. We spent a lot of time together down in the basement at Ma's place, listening to music, goofing off and drinking beer. As a teenager, I wasn't old enough to purchase my own beer. So whenever I wanted to get my hands on some I asked an adult named Bob Huff, who dated a classmate of mine named Debbie McCune, to buy it for me. We worked out an ingenious system too.

When the weekend rolled around, I put a sufficient amount of cash along with a note describing what I wanted inside Ma's mailbox. Then, as if spies working on a covert mission, I telephoned Debbie and said, "The money is in the mailbox." Later that evening, after Bob picked Debbie up at her parents' home, but before they went out on their date, they drove by Ma's place and picked up the cash along with my note from inside the mailbox. They then drove to the Loft, which was Osseo's only liquor store, and purchased the beer for me. I usually purchased Bosch, which was the cheapest beer on the market. The price for a six-pack was 97 cents, plus four cents sales tax.

Once Bob purchased the beer for me, he and Debbie drove back to Ma's place and rolled up beside the mailbox. Debbie then placed the six-pack or twelve-pack of beer inside the mailbox before they drove away. It was a flawless system that always worked. We only stopped using the system after I turned 18 and was able to purchase beer on my own. After the deliveries were completed, I patiently waited until after nightfall before removing the beer from the mailbox and placing it beside a basement window. Then I went inside the house and down into the basement where I opened the window and brought the beer inside. I then placed the warm beer inside a refrigerator until later at night.

After attending a sporting event, going to a Sage Dance at the City Hall Building, or doing something else altogether, I returned to Ma's place with a friend of mine to drink the beer. Sometimes the friend was Wendell Pederson or Del Van Blaricom. Other times it was

Robert Kershner or Terry Schimmelpfennig who accompanied me back to the basement. However, more often than not it was John Back who did so. We spent a lot of weekends down in the basement drinking beer and watching *Saturday Night Live* on a black-and-white television set. Looking back on the show now, many of the skits on the show were silly, but we thought they were hilarious at the time.

Although most of our time together was spent hanging out down in the basement at Ma's place, Yogi and I went on one memorable road trip to Union Grove, Wisconsin. While watching *ABC's Wide World of Sports* on television, I heard an ad on the television telling us that the Summer Nationals Drag Racing Championships would be held in Union Grove, Wisconsin, a city approximately 275 miles south of Osseo. John and I both knew Big Daddy Don Garlits was the most famous Drag Racer in the world, and that he had been featured on television countless times. After learning Big Daddy was going to participate, we decided then and there to attend the races.

It just so happened that Yogi had a brother who lived in Union Grove, and that meant we had a place to stay. After letting our mothers know of our plans, we hurriedly packed a change of clothes, filled the Pinto up with a tank of gas and took off for Union Grove. We thought to bring enough money for gas and food. However, in our irresponsible teenage haste, we neglected to bring enough money for admission to the drag races. Once we realized we didn't have enough money to pay for our admission and watch the races the conventional way, we attempted to sneak inside and watch them for free. Yogi and I walked along the fenced-off area for some time until we came across a small opening that was barely large enough for us to crawl under. After we quickly looked around to make sure nobody was watching, I crawled under the fence and then Yogi did the same.

For an instant or so we thought we had succeeded. However, before we took five steps a security guard yelled at us to stop. Out of fear more than anything else, we did as we were told. After a few stern questions, the security guard ordered us to crawl back under the fence and warned us that if he caught us attempting to sneak inside again he would have us arrested. We did as instructed and crawled back under the fence before quickly walking away. So all we actually managed to experience on our road trip to the Summer Nationals was listen to the roar of the engines and smell the burning tires from outside the fenced-off location where the Summer Nationals took place. When the races ended, it didn't really matter to us that we never saw Big Daddy Don Garlits. What was important was that we experienced our first road trip and managed to have a blast in the process.

When John Back and I weren't hanging out in the basement at Ma's place, we spent time at a tiny trailer house in Eddie Barber's Trailer Court that was rented by a hippie named Steve Matysik. The trailer that Steve rented was located in the same trailer park where Yogi lived, and that was how we met him. Steve was a bass guitar player and we used to stop by and listen while he practiced. Steve's Trailer, as the place came to be known, was the best place in town for hippies, hoodlums and other outsiders to hang out together and get wasted. It was at Steve's Trailer where I smoked my first marijuana, and for a brief time at least, getting high at Steve's Trailer became a regular weekend occurrence. Steve never told us where he purchased the pot and we never asked as that would have been an uncool thing to do.

Steve had an adult cat named Kitty that we used to get high from time to time. We took a toke of our smoke and then held Kitty still as we exhaled the smoke into his face. When Kitty got high, he stood and stared at inanimate objects such as a doorknob or a shoelace. Other times Kitty just stared into space for long periods of time. Of course, in our stoned state of mind, we always thought it was funny to watch Kitty as he stared off into the void. Eventually, I gave up smoking pot, but for a couple of years, it was a regular part of my weekend activities. Yogi and I gradually drifted apart. However, I have only fond memories of our time spent together. John Back was truly the funniest person that I have ever known.

After finishing a second can of ice-cold Walter's beer, I decided it was time to head back to my hotel room. So I paid my tab, said goodbye to the bartender and left the Northwoods Brew Pub. While driving out of the parking lot I decided to take a short spin past the high school. As with nearly everything else about the community where I once lived, the school that I attended in my youth had been replaced by a newer an larger building. As impressive as the new edifice was, I felt nostalgic for the past and the older school building that I attended from first through twelfth grade. After less than a minute's glance at the magnificent new school building, I left for my hotel where I eventually settled in for the night. Before falling asleep, though, I spent a lot of time reminiscing about my school years.

ORANGE AND BLACK FOREVER

Two blocks to the north of Ma's place stood our school, a large brick structure with a sign attached to the front that read Osseo Community Schools. The school building wasn't one of multiple schools in the community, it was the only school in the community, and kids from kindergarten through the twelfth grade attended classes inside the building. For several years, the students in Osseo attended Lincoln Hill School. However, that school burned to the ground in 1953. Work on a new school building began immediately, and through hard work, proper planning and a little bit of luck, the new school building was officially opened in time for the start of classes in 1954.

Shortly after I moved to Osseo, the school district merged with the school district covering the Village of Fairchild and came to be called the Osseo-Fairchild School District. With consolidation complete, high school students from Fairchild began attending classes in the City of Osseo in 1968. Although the official name of the school district changed when consolidation occurred, the sign reading Osseo Community Schools remained attached to the front of the school for several years. Even as a young kid, I realized it was wrong to leave that sign in place and wondered what the students from the Village of Fairchild thought about it: whether it made them feel like outsiders or even second-class students.

A new elementary school was eventually constructed in Osseo, and it opened for instruction in 1974. At that time, the school near Ma's place was converted into a junior high and high school. In time, the Osseo-Fairchild School District approved a referendum to build both a new high school and middle school. The Osseo-Fairchild High School and Osseo-Fairchild Middle School were officially dedicated at the start of the 2002 school year. Years later, the school district decided to close the elementary school in Fairchild and bus all of the students to Osseo. At that time, the name of the elementary school in Osseo was changed to the Osseo-Fairchild Elementary School.

The Osseo-Fairchild School District changed the school's nickname from the Chieftains to the Thunder in 2011. Osseo-Fairchild was the first public school in Wisconsin to make such a change in response to a state law passed the previous year that provided for individuals offended by school nicknames depicting American Indians to petition the Department of Public Instruction. The name Thunder was not among the four choices initially made available in a district-wide vote. Those choices were: Bengals, Dragons, Osprey and Phoenix. All four of those choices were rejected by the voters. It was a write-in campaign that resulted in the Thunder receiving the most votes.

A new logo was developed to correspond with the new nickname that represented a Scandinavian-looking character wielding an instrument similar to Mjølnir, the magical hammer used by Thor the Thunderer in Norse mythology. I was not living in the area when the school district changed the nickname. However, throughout the process, I was keenly aware that the issue deeply divided the community. Finally, although the nickname was changed to Thunder, the school district elected to maintain the school colors of orange and black.

When I began school in the first grade, my teacher was an amazing instructor named Solvie Finstad. As if yesterday, I remember my first day of school when I was delivered to her classroom by my brother Jeff. Miss Finstad looked at me and asked, "Well, what is your name, then?" I proudly responded, "My name is Daniel Ray Severson!" Miss Finstad chuckled at the boisterous response before pointing me to the desk where I was assigned to sit that year. School was difficult for me in the beginning. I couldn't print my name or any of the letters of the alphabet on that first day. Nor did I know how to write or identify any numbers.

Soon enough though, I was on top of the subject matter and could print my name and the letters in the alphabet. I also mastered all the numbers used when counting and doing basic arithmetic. By the end of the first grade I was able to read and write as well as any of my classmates. However, as early as the first grade I had a problem with the structure of the classroom. I didn't enjoy the rules that said I was only "allowed" to speak and move about with "permission" to do so from Miss Finstad.

What I liked best about going to school was playing with other kids at recess. I had never enjoyed so many people to play with in my life up to that point! I got along with all of the other students, but my best friends were three farm kids named Rodney Beam, Matt Cochran and Randy Kelly. As early as the first grade, I recognized a not so subtle distinction between the kids who lived in Osseo and those who lived in the country. What the students from Osseo thought of us I never knew, but I thought that the kids who lived in Osseo didn't have as much imagination. They tended to engage in organized forms of play with predetermined rules; games that other people had invented such as tag and kick ball. However, the kids that lived in the country engaged in forms of play that incorporated our physical surroundings. We seemed to prefer playing on the monkey bars, swings, slides and teeter-totters. It seemed to me that we were better at engaging in play that involved pretending, which allowed us to use our imagination rather than follow the rules.

My second year of elementary school was coming to a close when I moved from Pappy's farm to Osseo. My teacher in the second grade was a kind and gentle instructor named Marcella Isaacson. My third grade teacher was an equally wonderful instructor named Rita Jensen. The third grade was a memorable year for me in that I became friends with a kid named Terry Schimmelpfennig. Terry had moved from the nearby Village of Fairchild to Osseo around the time that I moved to Ma's place. As soon as the year began, we hit it off. Unfortunately, just before the school year ended, Terry moved back to Fairchild, and I did not see him again until our freshman year of high school.

My first three years of grade school were enjoyable and productive in that I learned a lot and met several new friends. However, my fourth grade year teacher was a cruel and vindictive woman named Mary Frank. From the first day, she demonstrated blatant favoritism towards certain kids and open contempt for others; I belonged to the second group of students. I can still recall her physically and verbally abusing me throughout the school year. I thought I was the only student that she tormented when I was a fourth grader. However, I learned years later that she not only mistreated me, she also abused several other students in the same way. Needless to say, I did not enjoy the fourth grade and kept praying for the school year to end. Eventually, it did and I was finally free from the almost daily abuse.

One of my best friends in first grade was a fellow farmer's son named Randy Kelly. However, soon after I moved to Osseo, our once strong friendship drifted apart, and by the end of the fourth grade we hardly spoke to one another. I was no longer considered a member of that friendly fraternity of future farmers that I spent recess with in the first grade. Nevertheless, I was brought to tears one ordinary afternoon near the end of our summer vacation that year when I heard Randy had been killed in a farming accident. He was only 11 years old when the Farmall C tractor he was operating rolled over and crushed him to death. The date was August 13, 1969.

The tractor Randy was operating at the time of his accident didn't have a working starter, and that meant it had to always be parked on the side of a hill before the engine was turned off. By parking the tractor on the side of a hill, the next person to use the tractor could start it by releasing the brake, which allowed the tractor to roll down the hill. As the tractor rolled down the hill, the operator placed the transmission in gear and released the clutch, which caused the engine to start. Randy Kelly got on the Farmall C tractor on the day of his accident and started the tractor in just such a way. However, once the tractor started, Randy apparently wasn't able to apply his foot to the brake before the tractor drove across a road and crashed into a ditch.

When the tractor hit the ditch it tipped over on Randy and pinned him underneath. Tragically, Randy's neck was broken and his chest was crushed when the tractor landed on him. He was killed instantly. A passing motorist saw the tipped-over tractor in the ditch and stopped to investigate. It was there that he discovered Randy's lifeless body. When I heard about Randy's death, I couldn't help but think how his death was eerily similar to the way Pappy was killed just three years earlier. Randy's untimely death hit me hard. It hit me very hard....

Fortunately, my fifth and sixth grade experiences were similar to the first, second and third grades before. I was free from the physical and emotional abuse that Miss Frank inflicted upon me, and I once again flourished at school. I had three wonderful teachers in the fifth grade named Anna Ruth Paulson, Louise Johnson and John Kennel. For one half of the year my home-room teacher was Mrs. Johnson, and the other half of the year it was Mrs. Paulson. Mrs. Johnson happened to be an accomplished pianist and probably spent more time and energy on music than was actually approved for her teaching plan. However, I sincerely believe that the other students and I benefitted as much by listening to the historically significant songs she sang as we would have from other instruction.

My sixth grade teachers were Adeline Goplin and John Kennel. Mrs. Goplin was a strict but effective educator. Were I asked to "grade" my elementary school teachers as they graded me, I would certainly give Mrs. Goplin an A+. She pushed me a lot throughout the year, and as a result I undoubtedly gained more knowledge on any number of topics than expected. Mr. Kennel taught science and math classes in both the fifth and sixth grades. He was my first male teacher, and in that capacity he proved to be an excellent role model. Mr. Kennel also succeeded in making math and science fun subjects to learn about, which some people might say was no easy task.

In the sixth grade, I began thinking of myself as something of a hippie and wore psychedelic shirts and black Beatle shoes to school. All my pants were striped bell bottoms. Also, Ma graciously allowed me wear my hair in a mop-top style that was a lot like that of the Beatles. It was during the sixth grade when the success of the various high school sports teams captured my attention. Soon, I was as much a fan of the Osseo-Fairchild Chieftains as anyone in the school. I attended all of the home basketball and football games as well as most of the wrestling matches. However, I was much less interested in watching the baseball games or track and field and golfing events.

The most exciting team that I followed while growing up in Osseo was the boys basketball team that played in 1971. The team's starting lineup was comprised of seniors Steve Rogness, Ron Johnson, Mike Nelson, Donnie Laufenberg and Gale Johnson. Junior Bob Kutchera was their sixth man. Other players contributed to the success of the team as well. The Chieftains were undefeated through regular season play and compiled a perfect 18 and 0 record. They continued their winning ways as the first round of Wisconsin Interscholastic Athletic Association (WIAA) regional play got underway.

In the first game, the Osseo-Fairchild Chieftains defeated the Fall Creek Crickets by a score of 89 to 72. The game was held on Friday, February 26, 1971. With the win, their record improved to 19 and 0. In the other game that night, the Altoona Railroaders defeated the Augusta Beavers by a score of 85 to 56. The following night the Chieftains faced the Railroaders and defeated them by a score of 72 to 54. With their win, the Chieftains improved to 20 and 0 and advanced to the regional tournament scheduled for the following weekend in Cadott, Wisconsin. I was able to attend the tournament thanks to the kindness of a gentleman named Larry Gomsrud and his wife Darliene, who invited me to ride to Cadott with them.

In the regional semi-finals, the Osseo-Fairchild Chieftains defeated the Owen-Withee Blackhawks by the lopsided score of 105 to 63. With the win, Osseo-Fairchild's already impressive record improved to 21 and 0. In the other game that night, the Cornell Chiefs defeated the Blair Cardinals by a score of 53 to 51. The following night, in the regional tournament championship, the Osseo-Fairchild Chieftains rolled over the Cornell Chiefs by the impressive score of 87 to 56. With the win, the Chieftains improved to 22 and 0 and advanced to the sectional tournament that was held in Marshfield, Wisconsin, the following weekend.

Unfortunately, the Osseo-Fairchild Chieftains lost to the Rhinelander Hodags in the sectional semifinal game that was played on Friday, March 12, 1971. The final score was 79 to 70. In the other semifinal game the Wausau East Lumberjacks defeated the Stratford Tigers by a score of 77 to 64. In the consolation game the following night, the Osseo-Fairchild Chieftains played the Stratford Tigers and won by the dominating score of 94 to 75. In the championship game the Wausau East Lumberjacks defeated the Rhinelander Hodags by a score of 86 to 80. By winning the tournament, the Lumberjacks advanced to the state tournament in Madison, Wisconsin.

In the days, weeks, months and even years that followed the loss, a lot of basketball fans expressed their sentiments about what happened. A highly respected journalist named Ron Buckli wrote that the primary reason Rhinelander won the game was because they completed "a deadly barrage of 21 straight free throws without a single miss." A lot of fans shared his point of view. I took pride in the fact that the fans who followed the basketball team that year were anything but sore losers. However, there were a few legitimate complaints about the tournament format. The WIAA adopted a one-class format for the state high school basketball tournament in 1940, and the result was that every high school in the Wisconsin–regardless of the size of their enrollment or the population of their school district–competed in the same class. So when the basketball tournament began in 1971, the Osseo-Fairchild Chieftains had to play against teams from more populous cities with significantly larger student enrollments.

In what I have always thought was a cruel twist of fate, the WIAA tournament switched from that one-class format to a two-class format in 1972. For several years parents, adults students and faculty alike have discussed what might have happened had the change occurred one year earlier. The general consensus was–and always will be–that had the WIAA made its decision to expand the tournament from the one-class format to a two-class format in advance of the 1971 season, the basketball team would have not only made it to the tournament, they would likely have won the state championship.

After finishing elementary school, I entered junior high school, which consisted of the seventh and eighth grades. I began wearing my hair longer and parted it down the middle. To keep the my hair from falling in my face, I wore a leather headband. I wore simple cotton shirts, blue jeans and a pair of leather boots. We always remained in one classroom in grade school. However, in junior high we moved around to different classrooms throughout the day. That significantly changed the way the students interacted with one another. We met in the hallway between classes and engaged in all kinds of conversations with other students throughout the day. I remember loving the added freedom that came with junior high school.

History was taught by a gentleman named Robert Boernke. He was the strictest teacher I ever had, including grades one through college. However, he was also fair to everyone, and from my perspective, he was an excellent instructor who I greatly respected. The same was true for Virginia Olson, my junior high math teacher. Mrs. Olson was consistently firm but always fair, and knowledgeable in the field of mathematics. My science teacher was named Jack Wolter, and my English teachers were Agnes Amundson and Fern Herrick. There were other teachers that taught both junior high and high school classes as well. Physical Education classes were separated by gender in the 1970s, with Harold Mulhern teaching the boys and Betty Ward teaching the girls. A gentleman named Paul Muus taught music, and an eccentric individual named Carl Bong taught art.

Mr. Bong's older brother was a real-life hero from World War II by the name of Richard Bong. Foremost among his many significant honors, Major Bong received the Congressional Medal of Honor. He was credited with shooting down 40 Japanese aircraft and was the nation's top flying ace in the war. Unfortunately, Major Bong was killed while testing a new fighter jet in California a short time before World War II ended. His death was front-page news across the USA, sharing front headline space with reports of the atomic bombing of Hiroshima. As an artist, Mr. Bong spent a substantial amount of his work day creating various forms of sculpture in tribute to his brother.

After junior high, I began my high school years. One of the things I was looking forward to as my freshman year began was reuniting with my old friend Terry Schimmelpfennig. I knew that he was one of the students from Fairchild who would be attending high school in Osseo. Unfortunately, things didn't happen as I had envisioned. Right from the start I noticed that Terry had changed a lot since the third grade. He undoubtedly noticed the same thing about me. We hung out again for a few days, but eventually, Terry started hanging out with another group of students and we drifted apart. A couple of years later, Terry dropped out of high school and we lost all contact with one another, just as we had after the third grade.

Early in the 2000s, I was searching the internet for information about classic muscle cars. While doing so I saw a name that immediately caught my attention. The name was Schimmelpfennig. I sent him a message and it was Terry. We were both older, if not wiser by then, and once we reconnected we vowed to stay in touch via the internet. We did too! We regularly exchanged e-mails in which we discussed various topics of mutual interest. I also made a point of having at least one in-person visit with Terry every time I returned to Osseo. One of the first things I observed during our initial visit was that he had not grown conventional in his thinking.

Although well into his fifties when we reconnected, Terry still lived what can only be described as the life of a bohemian. For the most part, I found him to be the same interesting, nonconformist hippie that I remembered from our high school days. However, there was one significant difference; Terry's once jet-black, shoulder length hair, had turned completely gray. Something else I realized right away was that he was every bit as intelligent as I remembered. Although Terry didn't graduate from high school, he was surprisingly well versed on a wide range of subjects.

Over several shots of Jack Daniel's and even more bottles of beer, Terry shared interesting stories of times spent living in California and other places, before settling down near the Village of Fairchild. He lived on a stretch of property that he inherited from his grandmother. During that first visit, I learned that Terry and his wife lived in a house that he built for his mother, shortly before she passed away. Throughout several subsequent e-mail exchanges, I reluctantly came to accept that Terry wasn't the most responsible man I had known. He seldom held the same job for very long, and he was frequently unemployed for extended periods of time.

Suffice it to say, Terry wasn't the first person I would contact when I found myself in need of assistance with an important matter of some kind. However, he was absolutely the first person I reached out to whenever I found myself wanting an unorthodox perspective on a particular subject of interest to me. I sincerely believe most of the people who had the pleasure of knowing Terry would agree that he excelled at thinking outside the box. Unfortunately, our renewed friendship didn't last as long as I would have liked. Terry Allen Schimmelpfennig passed away from lung cancer at his home in rural Fairchild, Wisconsin, on March 11, 2022. His cremated remains are buried at Hillcrest Cemetery, located in Price, Wisconsin.

Work is overrated.
Terry Schimmelpfennig

The Principal at Osseo-Fairchild High School was a man named John

Leadholm. Most of the students referred to him as "Chopper" behind his back. However, nobody called him that to his face. He was as tough as nails. Fortunately, he was also an exceptionally fairminded principal. As far as I could tell, Mr. Leadholm didn't care if a student was an athlete, a teacher's pet, a hoodlum or the child of a faculty member; he dealt with all of the students in the same harsh but fair manner. There were too many teachers in high school to list them all name by name. However, some of them had a profound and lasting impact on my life that bears mentioning.

One of my favorite high school teachers was James Rapp, who taught history classes. He was an extremely effective instructor who made learning about history both fun and exciting, and I took every class of his that I could. Another teacher that I greatly admired was Darwin Smith, who taught psychology and biology classes. He was also the coach for the wrestling team. I wouldn't ordinarily mention the fact that he was a coach but for the fact that Mr. Smith contracted polio earlier in life, which caused his right leg to atrophy. He had an extremely muscular upper body and left leg, but the right leg was tiny in comparison. However, in the same way that Ma never let her disabilities hold her back, Mr. Smith never let his disability get in the way of living his life to the fullest.

During my senior year, the Osseo-Fairchild Chieftains football team was an impressive juggernaut. They ended the regular season with a perfect 9 and 0 record. However, due to a less-than-perfect selection process developed by the WIAA, they were not selected to participate in the four-team Class C playoffs held that year. Ironically, one of the teams that was selected to play was the Mondovi Buffaloes, a team the Osseo-Fairchild Chieftains defeated earlier that season. It didn't seem fair that the undefeated Chieftains were left out of the playoffs when a team they defeated was selected to participate.

The main complaint about the unfairness of the selection process had to do with the different types of conferences in Wisconsin. Three of the four teams selected for the playoffs came from closed conferences in which the teams did not play against teams from other conferences. Another complaint was that there were more teams and conferences in Class C than in Class B, thus making it mathematically much more difficult for a school to make the Class C playoffs than the Class B playoffs. No playoff selection system is perfect. However, a lot of the coaches, players, students, parents and sports reporters alike all thought the unbeaten Osseo-Fairchild Chieftains got the proverbial shaft when they weren't selected for the playoffs that year.

I've often mused over another reason why the football team might not have been selected during our senior year. Specifically, because one of the team's best players, Wendell Pederson, was unable to play as a result of an automobile accident he experienced over the Labor Day weekend. The accident happened on September 4, 1976. My friends Wendell Pederson, Del Van Blaricom and I had been cruising around the back roads of Osseo in Wendell's 1974 Chevy Nova on the day of the accident. As was almost always the case in those days, we had a six-pack of ice-cold beer with us inside the car. Later, we purchased a bottle of blackberry flavored brandy that we consumed down in the basement at Ma's place. After finishing the brandy, Wendell decided to go to Foster to see his girlfriend Cindy Sell. Wendell dropped Del and I off at the fairgrounds and went on his way.

After spending some time with Cindy, Wendell left again for Osseo. Along the way, he was passed on the highway by an individual named Randy Maug. Wendell later intimated to me that he thought Randy was challenging him to a race, so he turned his car around and took off once again in the direction of Foster. While driving north towards Foster at a speed exceeding 100 miles an hour, Wendell lost control of his Chevy Nova while attempting to maneuver a slight curve in the highway. According to newspaper accounts, the Nova skidded off the road and struck a guardrail and some fencing. The car went airborne nearly 40 feet and rolled another 160 feet before coming to a stop. Wendell later explained to me that the primary reason he lost control of his car was because of a defective air shock that malfunctioned as he surpassed a speed of 100 miles per hour.

Immediately afterwards the authorities were called to the scene of the accident. Wendell was taken to Luther Hospital in Eau Claire, where he was treated for his serious injuries. He sustained a severe arm laceration, a badly fractured left leg and numerous contusions. At the time it was said he might never walk again. However, due in large part to his strength and physical fitness, Wendell managed to make a nearly full recovery. However, he still has a pronounced limp when he walks to this day. Although making the playoffs pales in comparison to the seriousness of Wendell's accident, I have often wondered whether his participation on the football team might have made them so dominant that the WIAA would have had no other option but to have selected the Osseo-Fairchild Chieftains as one of the four teams to make the playoffs that year.

Fortunately, the Osseo-Fairchild Chieftains football team fared a lot better the following year. Coach Duane Matye led his team to another undefeated season, ending the year with a perfect 10-0 record. But unlike the previous season when the undefeated Chieftains didn't receive a playoff birth, the 1977 team made the playoffs. The 4th ranked Osseo-Fairchild Chieftains played the 2nd ranked Grantsburg Pirates in one contest and the top ranked Coleman Cougars played the 3rd ranked Stanley-Boyd Orioles in the other contest. Osseo-Fairchild was victorious over Grantsburg and Stanley-Boyd defeated Coleman in those semifinal games.

When the Osseo-Fairchild Chieftains subsequently faced the Stanley-Boyd Orioles in the championship game, the Orioles dominated most of the first half. However, they were unable to score any points as their only touchdown was nullified by a clipping penalty. The Chieftains turned the tide of the game late in the second quarter when quarterback Van Vradenburg threw a perfectly executed 37-yard pass to Shawn Mulhern. That pass set up the Chieftains first touchdown which was subsequently scored off a 14-yard run by Joel Solie. Then, in the fourth quarter, Mark Rogness scored a second touchdown with an impressive one-yard run. The final score was 14-0. With the victory, the Osseo-Fairchild Chieftains won the school's first ever state football championship.

I have always considered myself fortunate to have had several truly outstanding teachers in high school. However, the faculty member who made the biggest impact on me wasn't even a teacher; it was my guidance counselor, Robert O. Johnson. His influence on my life was both profound and lasting. Mr. Johnson was a six-foot-six-inch tall man. However, as my real-life hero, I saw him as a man who walked at least 10 feet tall. He was usually even-tempered and demonstrated genuine concern for all of his students. More than any other member of the faculty at Osseo-Fairchild, I give Mr. Johnson credit for putting me on the pathway toward college and with it a better life. He not only persuaded me to apply for college, he even helped me fill out all of the necessary forms.

Graduation from the Osseo-Fairchild High School occurred on May 22, 1977. Sadly, Ma was unable to attend the ceremony, as it had become increasingly difficult for her to move about in her wheelchair. I have always believed in my heart that Ma would have found a way to attend had I not assured her it was alright for her not to attend the ceremony. Graduation day was a memorable and enjoyable time for me, and I soaked in every moment of the day. I can still remember the sense of accomplishment I felt as I walked across the stage to receive my diploma from Mr. Leadholm. As is the case with most people, I suspect, graduation from high school was an important moment in my life, and I took pride in the realization that from that day forward I could hold myself out to the world as a high school graduate.

CONCLUSION

The following morning, I awoke deciding I would return to Oklahoma after attending my brother's funeral. Although I had greatly enjoyed my brief visit to Osseo, I intuitively understood it was time to leave. I also understood that while Osseo would always be my hometown, so little of it was familiar to me that I had no reason to spend another day there. After checking out of the hotel I enjoyed a final breakfast at the Norske Nook. Then I took a final drive around Osseo before leaving for the South Beef River Lutheran Church. Along the way I began thinking about Larry and our limited interactions together.

When I was a kid, my friend Joe Keffer and I once rode our bikes the roughly ten mile distance from our homes in Osseo to his dairy farm. Larry was polite and friendly towards us when we unexpectedly arrived. However, because it was summertime and he had a lot of work to do, he didn't have much time for conversation. We visited for a while and then rode our bikes back to Osseo. Years later, after I obtained my driver license, I drove out to Larry's farm from time to time to visit with him–but only when he was milking his cows in the evening. Whenever I did so we engaged in long and enjoyable visits about a number of subjects as he patiently milked his herd of cows.

A word that accurately described Larry is eccentric. He was truly one of the most unique individuals that I have ever known. One thing that always amazed me about Larry was how up to date on current events he was in spite of his hermit-like lifestyle. Without access to the internet or cable television–even without so much as a telephone to connect him to the outside world, Larry was keenly aware of what was going on locally as well as at the state level in Madison. He also knew what was going on in Washington, D.C. and around the world.

From my perspective, the conversations we engaged in were never dull. He sometimes expressed interesting, albeit unorthodox points of view on the subjects we talked about and that made our conversations that much more enjoyable. I often wondered where Larry obtained all of his information. It wasn't until several years later that I learned from his daughter Jessica that Larry was, as Jessica said, a voracious reader of magazines. Over the years I gradually came to realize there was much about my oldest brother that I never knew.

Fortunately, Larry's funeral was a dignified ceremony. The pastor was truly skilled at painting him in the most favorable light possible without being either disingenuous or dishonest. The pastor openly acknowledged that Larry was not a religious man, but skillfully added that he undoubtedly recognized God's omnipresence in his pastures of plentiful crops and herds of healthy livestock. As I heard the pastor speak those eloquent words I thought how fitting they were. He was telling us that Larry belonged to the church of the blue sky and that his communion with God was realized in the rugged beauty of that which surrounded him on his dairy farm every day of his life.

After the funeral service, when everyone had left for the gravesite where Larry would finally be laid to rest, I glanced around inside the beautiful sanctuary of South Beef River Lutheran Church one last time. After a moment of quietude and personal reflection, I slowly walked outside, got inside my car and began my drive back to Oklahoma. I looked forward to seeing my beautiful wife Ana Maria once again. Throughout the long drive home, I thought about the many distant memories I had experienced anew while visiting Osseo and reminded myself they were all precious to me in their own way. I promised to keep them close to my heart for the rest of my life.

The End

Made in United States
Orlando, FL
13 December 2023